Introducing

Microsoft Word

FOR

WINDOWS 2.0

KEIKO PITTER

Mitchell **McGRAW-HILL**

New York St. Louis San Francisco Auckland Bogotá Caracas
Lisbon London Madrid Mexico Milan Montreal New Delhi Paris
San Juan Singapore Sydney Tokyo Toronto Watsonville

Mitchell **McGRAW-HILL**
Watsonville, CA 95076

Introducing Microsoft Word for Windows 2.0

3 4 5 6 7 8 9 0   SEM SEM   9 0 9 8 7 6 5 4

ISBN 0-07-051586-7

Sponsoring editor: Roger Howell
Editorial assistant: Laurie Boudreau
Technical reviewer: Laurie Boudreau
Director of production: Jane Somers
Production supervisor: Leslie Austin
Project manager: Gary Palmatier, Ideas to Images
Interior designer and illustrator: Gary Palmatier
Cover designer: Christy Butterfield
Composition: Ideas to Images
Printer and binder: Semline, Inc.

Library of Congress Card Catalog No. 92-82710

Contents

3 Advanced Editing Features

4 Graphics and Columns 77

Introduction

INTRODUCING MICROSOFT WORD FOR WINDOWS 2.0

A word processing program is a computer program that helps you create, change, and print text. Word processing simplifies the mechanics of preparing documents while freeing you to focus on the process of writing.

Introducing Microsoft Word for Windows 2.0 acquaints you with the essential information necessary to create simple to sophisticated documents. Working within the graphical environment of Windows, Word commands and features are presented to increase user knowledge and expertise. This manual is designed to get the user comfortable with the essentials of Word for Windows and feel confident exploring the program's capabilities.

Using This Module

To use this book, an IBM PC or compatible computer with a floppy disk drive, a mouse, Windows 3.1 software, and Microsoft Word for Windows 2.0 software are required. A blank, formatted floppy diskette is also required. If your configuration deviates from this, consult your instructor.

This module is designed to assist you as you complete each lesson. Lessons begin with goals that are listed under the heading *Objectives*. Key terms are introduced in ***bold italic*** type; text to be typed by the user is shown in **bold**. Also, keep in mind the following:

■ This symbol is used to indicate the user's action.

▶ *This symbol is used to indicate the screen's response.*

Alternative: Presents an alternative keystroke "shortcut."

NOTE: This format is for important user notes and tips.

PRACTICE TIME

These brief drills allow the user to practice features previously discussed.

Finally, a command summary, a series of projects, and a glossary of key terms are found at the end of the book.

Creating Documents

OBJECTIVES

Upon completing the material presented in this lesson, you should understand the following aspects of Microsoft Word:

- ☐ **Starting Microsoft Word**
- ☐ **Word processing terminology**
- ☐ **Giving Microsoft Word commands**
- ☐ **Entering text**
- ☐ **Saving a file on a disk**
- ☐ **Moving through a document**
- ☐ **Selecting text**
- ☐ **Deleting selected text**
- ☐ **Replacing selected text**
- ☐ **Moving/copying selected text**
- ☐ **Inserting text in an existing document**
- ☐ **Checking the spelling**
- ☐ **Using the thesaurus**
- ☐ **Printing the document**

STARTING OFF

Before starting Microsoft Word, you start the Microsoft Windows program.

■ Start the Windows program. Make sure the Program Manager is the only window displayed on the screen.

▶ *The installation procedure for Microsoft Word created a program group icon for Word for Windows in the Program Manager window (Figure 1-1).*

Figure 1-1

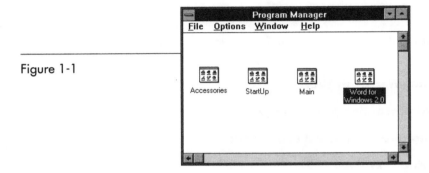

■ Maximize the Program Manager window.

■ Open the Microsoft Word window by double-clicking on the Word for Windows group icon.

▶ *The Word for Windows window, similar to the one in Figure 1-2, is displayed.*

Figure 1-2

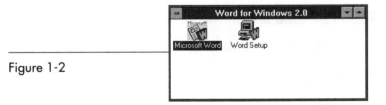

The Word program group window has two application icons—the Microsoft Word program and Word Setup. To start Microsoft Word, double-click on the Microsoft Word icon.

■ Launch the Microsoft Word program by double-clicking on the Microsoft Word icon.

▶ *The Microsoft Word application window is displayed, as shown in Figure 1-3.*

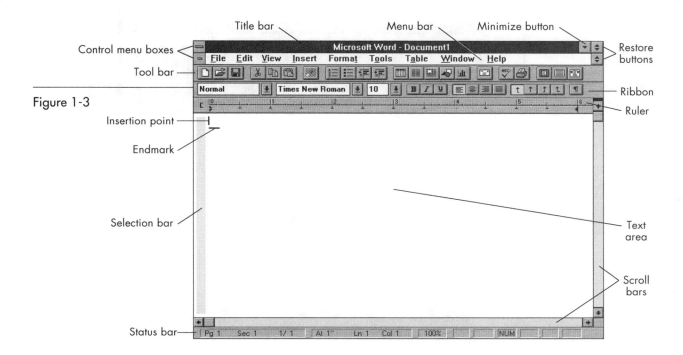

Figure 1-3

The Microsoft Word application window has all the basic components of a Windows window—a title bar; a menu bar; a control-menu box; minimize, maximize, and restore buttons; and scroll bars. There are additional elements such as the tool bar, ribbon, and ruler under the menu bar and the status bar at the bottom. These are explained in just a while.

You might notice that there are two restore buttons and two control-menu boxes. This is because, on the screen right now, there are two windows displayed: the Microsoft Word application window and a new document window. The new **document window** is contained within the **workspace**, or the area between the menu bar and the status bar, of the Microsoft Word **application window**, and the new document window is already maximized.

■ Restore the document window by clicking on the lower restore button.

▶ *The document window is restored, as shown in Figure 1-4.*

Now you can see the document window more distinctly. The workspace for Windows can contain up to nine documents if your computer has enough available memory. You might notice that the title bar of the Microsoft Word application window displays "Microsoft Word," and that of the document window contains the name of the document, DOCUMENT1.

■ Maximize the document window.

▶ *Notice that the title bar is changed to Microsoft Word - Document1 and that the new document window fills the workspace.*

Figure 1-4

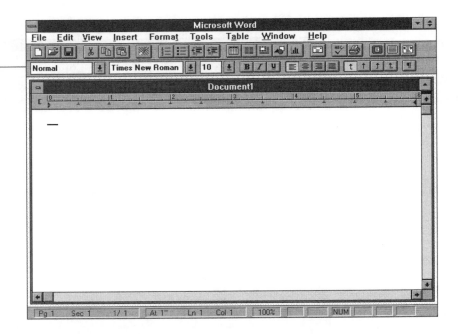

The **menu bar**, located beneath the title bar, contains nine menu options. Microsoft Word commands are accessed either by clicking on the desired menu option or by pressing the [Alt] key and the key of the underlined letter in the menu option you want. When you select a menu option, a menu containing the commands, called a **drop-down menu**, appears below the option. You can make a selection in the drop-down menu by clicking on a command or pressing the key of the underlined letter in the command.

Under the menu bar is the **tool bar**. It contains tools that give you quick access to frequently used commands. Tools are explained as each is encountered in the lessons.

The **ribbon**, located beneath the tool bar, contains buttons that let you change the way text looks. For example, the first three buttons indicate the type of characters (typeface and size) currently used and the next three buttons are for bold, italic, and underline.

The **ruler** displays and allows you to change the margins, tabs, and indentation settings.

NOTE: The tool bar, ribbon, and ruler can be hidden from display.

The area below the ruler is now the **text area**. This is the area in which you can enter new text or graphics, review what you have already entered, or change what is there. Of course, because you have not entered anything yet, this area is blank. The blinking vertical bar is the **insertion point**, and the underscore is the **endmark**. The insertion point shows the position in the workspace where your entries are made, and the endmark identifies the end of your document.

Along the left side of the text area is an unmarked area called the **selection bar**. It helps you select text with the mouse. When the mouse pointer is in the text area, it turns into an **I-beam**. However, when it is in the selection bar, it turns into a right-pointing arrow (↗).

At the bottom of the screen is the **status bar**. It displays the following information about the page that contains the insertion point: the page number, the section number, the total number of pages from the beginning of the document followed by the total number of pages in the whole document, the position of the insertion point measured from the top edge of the page, the line number, and the column number calculated by counting the number of characters between the insertion point and the left margin. The status bar also shows the level of magnification, which should now be 100%, as well as the status of several keys on your computer, such as [Caps Lock] and [Num Lock], and of various Word features.

MICROSOFT WORD COMMANDS

As mentioned earlier, a command can be entered using the mouse or the keyboard, in the same manner as you can with any Windows application. You will notice that some commands are **toggles**, which means the command turns a feature on or off each time you enter it. When a toggle feature is on, a checkmark appears before the command option in the menu, and the checkmark disappears when the feature is turned off. Some other commands display a **dialog box** where you are required to enter additional information, such as the name to call a document.

Many commands offer you a shortcut. These commands can be entered by clicking on a tool button or pressing a key in combination with the [Ctrl], [⇧ Shift], or [Alt] keys. When you see [⇧ Shift]+[F12], for example, you are to hold down the key marked [⇧ Shift] and press the [F12] function key; when you see [Ctrl]+[X], you hold down the [Ctrl] key and press [X]. Combination shortcut keys appear next to the corresponding command in the drop-down menu. Where available, these tool buttons and combination shortcut keys are given in this manual.

ENTERING TEXT

To enter text, use your keyboard just as you would a typewriter. As you enter a character, it appears at the insertion point, and the insertion point moves to the right one position. However, unlike the keyboard on a typewriter, this keyboard does not require entry of a carriage return as you fill up a line on the screen. Just keep on typing, because when the cursor gets beyond the right margin, it will reappear at the left margin setting, one line down. When you come to the end of a paragraph, the [←Enter] key must be pressed. The [←Enter] key breaks the line and moves the insertion point to the left margin, one line down. You have to press ⏎Enter once at the end of a paragraph, or press ⏎Enter twice if you want to insert a blank line between paragraphs in the text.

If your text fills up the screen, the text will **scroll** up: A new line will appear at the bottom of the screen, and the uppermost line will disappear from view.

Correcting Errors

If you make a mistake when you are typing text, you may delete unwanted characters by pressing the ←Backspace key, which is the left-arrow key found just above the ⏎Enter key. You can then retype the text.

Uppercase Letters

To enter uppercase letters, simply hold down the ⇧Shift (large up-arrow) key while you press the character—as you would on a typewriter. If you want to type several characters in uppercase, as when you enter a title, press the Caps Lock key, just as you would do with the Shift Lock key on a typewriter. To get back into lowercase, simply press Caps Lock again. When you enter certain special characters, you have to hold down the ⇧Shift key regardless of whether Caps Lock has been pressed.

P R A C T I C E   T I M E   1 - 1

Enter the following text.

Records of transactions, contracts, and inventories form the basis that allows business to be conducted in an orderly manner. Scribes have been used through the ages to produce copies of business contracts. Inventions that have lowered the cost or increased the speed for an individual to write a document have resulted in increased business productivity. These inventions include paper, pens, and the typewriter. The personal computer did not become a success until it became useful for business. Today, word processing is the most common business use of personal computers.

As you typed in this paragraph, you might have noticed the phenomenon called **wordwrap**. This means that as the text gets to the right margin, a word that is too long to fit on the line is moved down to the next line. Words are not split between two lines. This feature is included to make reading and text creation easier.

SAVING YOUR WORK

The text you have just entered is stored in the main memory of the computer. If you turn off the computer or if there is a power failure, you lose that text. That is why it is important that you save the file on a disk, not only when you quit Microsoft Word, but also frequently during your Microsoft Word session. Once a file is on a disk, it is permanently stored. Should there be a power failure, you can retrieve the most recent version of the file from the disk and continue with your work.

NOTE: This manual assumes that your data disk is in drive A. If you are using a drive other than A, substitute the appropriate drive in the instructions.

■ Make sure a formatted disk is in drive A.

When you save a file, you have two choices: you can use the Save command or the Save As command.

• If you use the Save command, the file is saved using the filename that appears on the title bar. If there already is a file by that name on the disk, the new file will replace the other file.

• If you use the Save As command, you type a new name for your file.

The first time you save a document, you are forced to use the Save As command no matter which save option you select. This is to be sure that you give a meaningful name to the document rather than the default name assigned by Microsoft Word.

As mentioned earlier, when you start a new file, Microsoft Word automatically gives it a default name, such as DOCUMENT1. When you save the file for the first time, you use the Save As command and give it a valid and more meaningful name. A valid name for the document, known as the ***filename***, is one to eight characters in length, followed by an optional extension. The extension is a period (.) and one to three additional characters. If you do not supply an extension, Microsoft Word automatically assigns the extension DOC. You can use any characters except spaces and the following characters: * ? , ; [ ] + = \ / : | < >. You cannot use a period except to separate the filename from the extension. Right now, use the name MYFILE to save this file on the disk in drive A.

■ Click on File in the menu bar and then on Save As.

Alternative: Press [F12] or click on the save tool button (⊞).

▶ *The Save As dialog box is displayed as shown in Figure 1-5.*

NOTE: The save tool button works the same way as the Save command. The file is saved using the current filename.

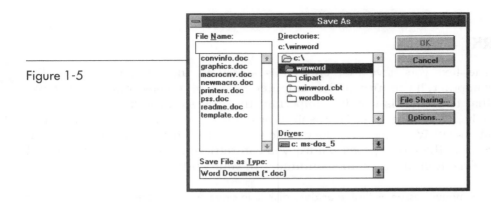

Figure 1-5

The insertion point is blinking in the File Name text box. Type the filename, but do not press ⏎Enter.

■   Type **MYFILE**, but do not press ⏎Enter.

You need to specify the location of your data disk.

■   Click on the down-arrow key at the right end of the Drives list box.

▶   *All available drives are displayed.*

■   Click on a: for drive A.

▶   *The Directories list box displays all directories currently on drive A. If you need to specify the directory, do so by clicking on the directory name.*

■   Complete the command by either clicking on the OK button or pressing ⏎Enter.

▶   *The Summary Info dialog box appears as shown in Figure 1-6.*

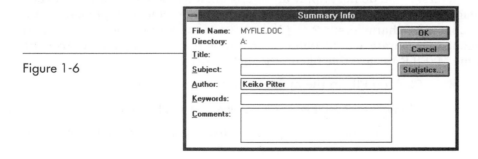

Figure 1-6

When you save a file for the first time, Word by default displays the Summary Info dialog box. Although you don't have to provide summary information to save a file (just press ⏎Enter), taking a minute to type information about the document—such as its title and subject—will help you locate the document more quickly when you need it later. This is useful if you work with many documents.

NOTE: You can provide summary information for a document at any time by choosing the Summary Info command from the File menu or selecting the Summary button in the Find File dialog box from the File menu.

■ With the insertion point in the Title text box, type **My File**, and then press Tab⇆.

▶ *The insertion point is in the Subject text box.*

■ Type **Hands-on Exercises**, and press Tab⇆ twice.

▶ *The insertion point is in the Keywords text box.*

■ Type **Lesson 1**.

NOTE: The name that appears in the Author text box is that of the registered owner of the software. Change the entry as appropriate.

■ Enter other information as appropriate.

■ When finished, complete the command by clicking OK or pressing ←Enter.

▶ *The file is saved to the disk in drive A.*

MOVING THROUGH THE DOCUMENT

Suppose, as you read what you typed earlier, you find a mistake or you decide to change the text. If the change you want to make is at the beginning of the text, and if you use the ←Backspace key to erase all unwanted characters starting at the insertion point, you will have to retype almost the whole text. This is no improvement over using a typewriter. A word processor has a better way. To make a correction such as this, you need to learn how to move through the document, which means you need to learn how to move the insertion point. Text is entered, deleted, or edited at the insertion point.

Using the Mouse

The insertion point may be moved by positioning the I-beam in the desired place and clicking the left mouse button once. If the desired text position has scrolled off the screen, bring it back to display by clicking on the scroll arrows on either end of the vertical scroll bar at the right. When you scroll the text display, however, the insertion point stays in its original position and does not move. Hence, you need to specify the insertion point.

■ Use the mouse to move the insertion point.

Using the Keyboard

To move the insertion point, use the four arrow keys located on the numeric keypad to the right of the main keyboard (or the arrow keys located between the main keyboard and the numeric keypad on extended keyboards). The insertion point will move in the direction of the arrow, one position at a time.

N O T E :   If you are using the numeric keypad, make sure Num Lock is turned off.

■   Press the ↑ key.

▶   *The insertion point moves up one line.*

■   Press the → key.

▶   *The insertion point moves to the right one position.*

If you have a long text, you cannot see all of it on the screen at any one time. As you press ↑ or ↓ repeatedly, the insertion point will keep moving up or down, forcing the screen to scroll. If you keep pressing ↑, the text will scroll down (new lines will appear at the top), and if you keep pressing ↓, the text will scroll up (new lines will appear at the bottom).

N O T E :   You will quickly learn that the movement of text on the screen is in the direction opposite to the label on the key. The ↑ key lets you view text that was above the screen, and the ↓ key brings into view text that was below the screen.

It is also possible to move the insertion point a little faster. All you have to do is hold down the key, and the key will keep repeating. If you hold down the ↓ key, the insertion point will zoom down the page. You can return the insertion point to the top of the page by using the ↑ key. You will notice, however, that you cannot move the insertion point past the beginning or end of the text.

You can move the insertion point to the left or right, one word at a time, by holding down the Ctrl key and pressing the ← and → keys, respectively.

N O T E :   On some computers, when giving a combination command with arrow keys, Num Lock must be turned off regardless of which set of arrow keys is used.

You can move the insertion point to the beginning of the document by pressing Ctrl+Home: Hold down the Ctrl key while you press the Home key. You can move the insertion point to the end of the document by pressing Ctrl+End. Table 1-1 lists various keystrokes for moving the insertion point.

TABLE 1-1

Key	Action
→	Moves one character to the right
←	Moves one character to the left
↑	Moves one line up
↓	Moves one line down
Ctrl + Home	Moves to the beginning of a document
Ctrl + End	Moves to the end of a document
Ctrl + →	Moves one word to the right
Ctrl + ←	Moves one word to the left
Home	Moves to the beginning of a line
End	Moves to the end of a line
Ctrl + ↑	Moves up one paragraph
Ctrl + ↓	Moves down one paragraph
Pg Up	Moves up one window
Pg Dn	Moves down one window

The text you see on the screen right now is not long enough for you to try all of these keys. Just remember them for the future.

P R A C T I C E   T I M E   1 - 2

1. Move the insertion point to the end and then to the beginning of the document.

2. Place the insertion point somewhere in the middle of the document.

3. Try other ways of moving the insertion point.

DELETING TEXT

As you recall, if you make a mistake in typing text, you can correct it immediately in this way:

- Press ←Backspace to remove unwanted characters.
- Type the correct text.

You may delete unwanted characters *anywhere* in the text by adding one step:

- Move the insertion point to the immediate right of the character you wish to delete.

- Press ⌫Backspace to erase unwanted characters.

- Type the correct text.

The ⌫Backspace key removes the characters to the left of the insertion point. You can delete text using the keyboard in other ways, too:

- Remove the character to the right of the insertion point by pressing the Del key.

- Remove the word before the insertion point by entering Ctrl+⌫Backspace: Hold down the Ctrl key and press ⌫Backspace.

- Remove the word after the insertion point by entering Ctrl+Del: Hold down the Ctrl key and press the Del key.

You can also delete a selected section of text.

SELECTING TEXT

You will now select the second sentence, which begins, "Scribes have..."

- Place the I-beam to the left of the character "S" of "Scribes have...," and then drag the mouse to highlight the entire sentence. To do this, hold down the left mouse button, move the mouse until the sentence is highlighted, and then release the button.

  Alternative: Position the insertion point anywhere in the sentence and then Ctrl+click: Hold down the Ctrl key and click the left mouse button.

▶ *The sentence is selected as shown in Figure 1-7.*

Figure 1-7

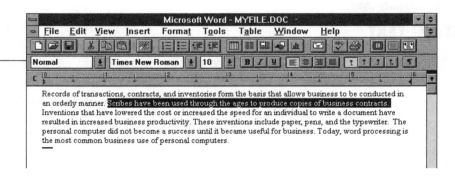

NOTE: If you selected the wrong text, click elsewhere on the screen or press an arrow key to deselect.

Another way to select text is by using the selection bar, which is an unmarked area along the left side of the text area. In the selection bar, the mouse pointer changes to a right-pointing arrow. Using the selection bar and mouse, you can select a line, paragraph, or entire document with one or two mouse clicks.

Table 1-2 shows ways of selecting text using the selection bar and mouse, as well as ways of selecting using the keyboard.

Deleting Selected Text

■   Press either ⟮←Backspace⟯ or ⟮Del⟯ to delete the selected text. Do not move the insertion point.

TABLE 1-2

Using Mouse	Selection
Double-click	Word
⟮Ctrl⟯+click anywhere in sentence	Sentence
Place pointer in the selection bar, point to line, and click	Line
Place pointer in the selection bar, point to paragraph, and double-click	Paragraph
⟮Ctrl⟯+click anywhere in the selection bar	Document

Using Keyboard	Selection
⟮⇧Shift⟯+⟮→⟯	One character to the right
⟮⇧Shift⟯+⟮←⟯	One character to the left
⟮⇧Shift⟯+⟮↑⟯	One line up
⟮⇧Shift⟯+⟮↓⟯	One line down
⟮⇧Shift⟯+⟮Home⟯	To the start of a line
⟮⇧Shift⟯+⟮End⟯	To the end of a line
⟮⇧Shift⟯+⟮Pg Up⟯	One screen up
⟮⇧Shift⟯+⟮Pg Dn⟯	One screen down
⟮⇧Shift⟯+⟮Ctrl⟯+⟮←⟯	To the start of a word
⟮⇧Shift⟯+⟮Ctrl⟯+⟮→⟯	To the end of a word
⟮⇧Shift⟯+⟮Ctrl⟯+⟮↑⟯	To the start of a paragraph
⟮⇧Shift⟯+⟮Ctrl⟯+⟮↓⟯	To the end of a paragraph
⟮⇧Shift⟯+⟮Ctrl⟯+⟮Home⟯	To the start of a document
⟮⇧Shift⟯+⟮Ctrl⟯+⟮End⟯	To the end of a document
⟮Ctrl⟯+⟮5⟯ (5 on the numeric keypad)	An entire document

Restoring Deleted Text

If you realize you didn't mean to remove the text after you've deleted it, you can restore it immediately by using the Undo command.

■   Click on Edit and then on Undo Typing.

Alternative: Press Ctrl+Z or click on the undo tool button. (▨).

▶   *The text is restored.*

P R A C T I C E   T I M E   1 - 3

Delete the second sentence again.

REPLACING TEXT

You can easily replace a word or phrase with different text.

■   Select the text "personal computer" in the next-to-last sentence.

■   Type **microcomputer**.

▶   *The highlighted text is deleted and replaced by what you typed.*

P R A C T I C E   T I M E   1 - 4

Change "microcomputer" back to "personal computer" in the text.

MOVING TEXT

You can also move selected text from one location to another. This is done using the Cut and Paste commands. When you *cut* text, the Cut command removes the selected text from a document and places the selection on the Windows *Clipboard*, which is a temporary storage place for information you want to transfer. You can then *paste*, or insert, the information where you specify.

Right now, you will move the last sentence.

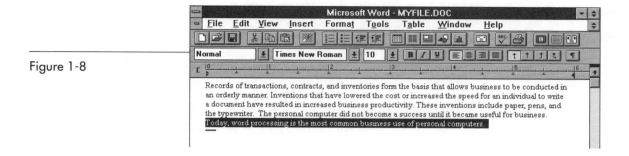

Figure 1-8

■ Select the last sentence, "Today, word processing is the most common business use of personal computers," as shown in Figure 1-8.

■ From the Edit menu, select Cut.

Alternative: Press Ctrl+X or click the cut tool button (▨).

▶ *The selected text disappears. It has been placed on the Clipboard.*

■ Move the insertion point to the space just before the fourth sentence, after the word "typewriter."

■ From the Edit menu, select Paste.

Alternative: Enter Ctrl+V or click the paste tool button (▨).

▶ *The text is placed at the insertion point position as shown in Figure 1-9. You may have to insert or delete spaces to make the sentence display correct.*

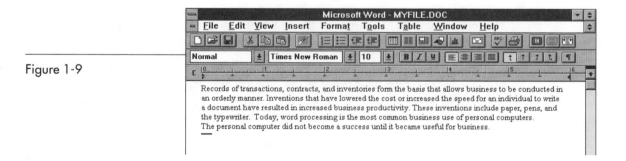

Figure 1-9

PRACTICE TIME 1 - 5

Move the sentence you just moved back to its original position.

INSERTING TEXT

If you need to insert a word in the middle of a sentence, or a sentence in the middle of a paragraph, position the insertion point where you want to begin inserting the text, and then look at the status bar. If you see the letters "OVR," press the Ins key. When you press Ins, the letters "OVR" disappear. Then you can start typing whatever you want to insert at the insertion point position.

When OVR is not on, Word is in **insert mode**, and any text in "front" of the insertion point (to the right) is pushed across the line to make room for your insertion. When OVR is on, however, Word is is **typeover mode**, and the character you type replaces the character the insertion point is on. Insert is a toggle command, which means the feature is turned on and off each time you press Ins.

■ Place the insertion point just before the word "Inventions" in the second sentence.

■ Insert the following text just as it appears (with spelling errors):

The earliest writing, cuneiform inscriptoins on on clay tablets, often kept business recrds.

CHECKING SPELLING

Microsoft Word can check your document for misspelled words, two occurrences of a word in a row, and certain types of capitalization errors. The spelling feature helps you proof the document on the screen by comparing each word in the document with a list of correctly spelled words, known as a **dictionary**. When you issue the Spelling command, the program scans the document, flags those words that are not in the dictionary, and, for each of these words, suggests words in the dictionary that you might have meant.

NOTE: If a word is not in the Microsoft Word dictionary, such as a proper name or a term that is special to a particular industry, the program will flag the word as misspelled. You have the option of adding the word to a custom dictionary. Once a word is added, additional occurrences of the same word are not flagged.

The program checks the entire document starting at the insertion point. If the insertion point is at the middle of the document, then when the program gets to the end of the document, Word will ask you whether you want to continue checking at the beginning of the document. If you do not want to check all of your document, select that part of document you want to check and then give the Spelling command.

You entered some words with spelling errors in the current document. You will now enter the Spelling command to correct these mistakes.

■ Position the insertion point at the beginning of the document.

■ From the T<u>o</u>ols menu, select <u>S</u>pelling.

Alternative: Click the spelling tool button ().

▶ *The Spelling dialog box is displayed as shown in Figure 1-10.*

Figure 1-10

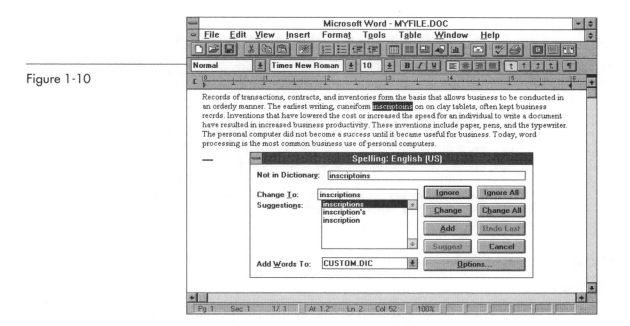

The word "inscriptoins" is highlighted in the document and appears in the Not in Dictionary text box. In the Suggestions list box, the word "inscriptions" is listed and highlighted. As the highlighted word, it also appears in the Change To text box. Because the highlighted word is the correct spelling, you tell Word to replace it in the document.

■ Click on the <u>C</u>hange button.

▶ *The correctly spelled word is inserted. Now the word "on" is highlighted in the document.*

N O T E : If you were to click on Change All instead, all instances of the same word subsequently found in your document are corrected.

Word now tells you that the word "on" is a repeated word, which means it appears twice in a row. You want to delete the second occurrence.

■ Click on the Delete button.

▶ *The second "on" is deleted. Now, the word "recrds" is highlighted.*

P R A C T I C E   T I M E   1 - 6

Replace the word "recrds" with the correctly spelled word. When the spell-check is finished, a dialog box appears to notify you. Respond accordingly.

If a word is flagged but is spelled correctly or a suggested spelling is not given, the word is not currently contained in the Microsoft Word dictionary. You can do one of four things: (1) Add the word to a custom dictionary by selecting the Add button, (2) tell Word to ignore the occurrence of this word this one time by clicking the Ignore button, (3) tell Word to ignore the occurrence of this word for the rest of the document by clicking the Ignore All button, or (4) edit the word manually. To edit the word manually, place the insertion point in the Change To text box using the mouse, edit the word, and then click the Change option.

After you finish entering text, you should always run it through the spelling checker. It does not catch all your mistakes—for example, if you use "their" for "there," because both words are correct spellings—but it is still a good aid in creating an accurate document.

THESAURUS

One more feature that is available in many word processors is the thesaurus. Many times, when you are writing a document, you need help finding a word so you can express yourself more clearly. The thesaurus displays synonyms and other words that point to the same idea.

Assume that in the current text (on the screen), you decide that the word "contracts" in the first sentence is not quite what you wanted to say.

■   Place the insertion point anywhere in the word "contracts."

■   From the T̲ools menu, select T̲hesaurus.

Alternative: Press ⟨⇧Shift⟩+⟨F7⟩.

▶   *The Thesaurus dialog box is displayed, as shown in Figure 1-11.*

Figure 1-11

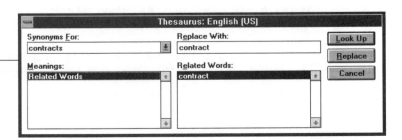

In the dialog box, Word is now saying that the word "contracts" does not appear in the thesaurus. However, it lists the singular form "contract" as a related word. You can look up a related word, in this case "contract," in the thesaurus.

■   Click on the Look Up button.

▶   *Both list boxes display various options for "contract."*

The Meanings list box displays different meanings of the word. This includes both noun and verb uses of the word. The list also includes an antonym, or the word with the opposite meaning, and other related words. The Synonyms list box on the right displays the words with the selected meaning. The highlighted word in the Synonyms list box also appears in the Replace With text box.

As you select different meanings in the Meanings list box, the content of the Synonyms list box changes to display words with the selected meaning. If you see the word you are looking for in the Synonyms list, select the word and then click the Replace button. For example, if the word you want to use is "agreement," select it by clicking on it and then clicking the Replace button. The word "contracts" in the text will be replaced by "agreement." If you did not find the word you are looking for in this list, you can continue the search by doing a Look Up on any of the words listed.

■   Select Cancel to exit the thesaurus.

P R A C T I C E   T I M E   1 - 7

Use the thesaurus to replace the singular word "contract" with "agreement." Because Microsoft Word inserts the singular word "agreement," you will have to enter an "s" at the end to make the word plural to agree with the rest of the sentence.

SAVING AN EXISTING FILE

Now that you've made several changes to your file, you should save it again. This time, you will save using the same filename.

■   Make sure the data disk is in drive A.

■   From the File menu, select Save.

Alternative: Press ⇧Shift+F12 or click the save tool button.

▶   *The current document replaces the one on the data disk.*

PREVIEWING TEXT

Before printing the text on a sheet of paper, you can view it on the screen. This is called ***previewing*** a text. Although there is a Preview command within the File menu, you will preview using the zoom-whole-page tool button.

N O T E :   The screen that is displayed from the Preview command in the File menu is different from the one you see when you use the zoom-whole-page tool button.

■   Click on the zoom-whole-page tool button (🔲).

▶   *A screen similar to Figure 1-12 is displayed.*

Figure 1-12

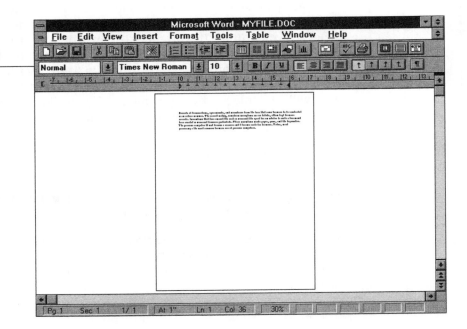

The screen displays how your page will look when it is printed. However, it is too small to see detail. You can enlarge the display.

■   Click on the zoom-page-width tool button (🔲).

▶   *The display is enlarged as shown in Figure 1-13.*

■   Click on the Zoom-100-percent tool button (🔲).

▶   *The display returns to normal view.*

If you are satisfied with what you see, you can proceed to print. However, if you are not satisfied, you can go back to editing the document without wasting a sheet of paper.

■   From the <u>V</u>iew menu, select <u>N</u>ormal to exit the preview mode.

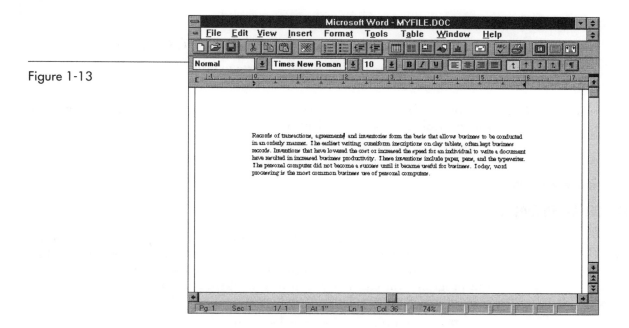

Figure 1-13

PRINTING TEXT

Now you will print the text.

■   Make sure your printer is turned on and is ready to use.

■   From the File menu, select Print.

Alternative: Press `Ctrl`+`⇧Shift`+`F12`.

▶   *The Print dialog box is displayed, as shown in Figure 1-14.*

■   Make sure the printer you are using appears next to "Printer:". If it does not, ask your instructor for instructions.

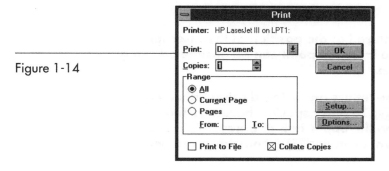

Figure 1-14

For now, do not change option settings.

■   Complete the command by clicking on OK or pressing `←Enter`.

▶   *The text for MYFILE starts to print.*

N O T E :   The print tool (⊞) gives you a convenient way to print. However, when you print using the print tool you cannot control the printing process.

ENDING LESSON 1

You should never quit Microsoft Word by just turning off your computer. Always exit to Windows and then properly quit Windows before shutting down your system. When you properly exit Microsoft Word and Windows, the program will caution you if any worksheet or other documents have been changed since they were last saved.

■   From the File menu, select Exit.

Alternative: Press `Alt`+`F4`.

▶   *If any open documents were changed since they were last saved, a cautionary dialog box appears, giving you a chance to save the document again. Select Yes or No accordingly.*

▶   *You return to Windows.*

■   Quit the Windows session.

■   Remove your data disk from the disk drive.

■   Turn off your computer and monitor.

S U M M A R Y

In this lesson, many of the terms and concepts that are necessary to use a word processor are introduced.

☐   **Text is entered at the position of the insertion point. The insertion point can be positioned using the mouse.**

☐   **Uppercase letters are entered using either `⇧Shift` or `Caps Lock`. To enter special characters that appear on the upper half of a key, `⇧Shift` must be held down, even if `Caps Lock` has been pressed.**

☐ **Words are not split between two lines but are placed complete on one line through a feature called wordwrap. You only press** `←Enter` **at the end of a paragraph or to insert a blank line.**

☐ **The insertion point can be moved using the keyboard or the mouse.**

☐ **Pressing** `Ins` **toggles OVR on and off. In OVR mode, the character you type replaces the one the insertion point is on, whereas when OVR is off, the character the insertion point is on and all characters to the right move over when text is entered.**

☐ **Text can be selected by pointing to the first character with the mouse, dragging the mouse until the text is highlighted, and releasing the mouse button.**

☐ **Text can also be selected using the selection bar and mouse as well as with the keyboard.**

☐ **A valid filename is one to eight characters in length, followed by an optional extension.**

☐ **When you save a file for the first time, you can enter information in the Summary Info dialog box. The information entered is used to identify and retrieve the file later.**

KEY TERMS

application window	I-beam	selection bar
Clipboard	insert mode	status bar
cut	insertion point	text area
dialog box	menu bar	toggle
dictionary	paste	tool bar
document window	previewing	typeover mode
drop-down menu	ribbon	wordwrap
endmark	ruler	workspace
filename	scroll	

COMMAND SUMMARY

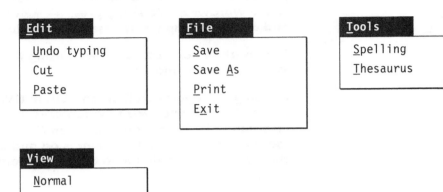

Edit
Undo typing
Cut
Paste

File
Save
Save As
Print
Exit

Tools
Spelling
Thesaurus

View
Normal

REVIEW QUESTIONS

1. Why should you not press ⏎Enter at the end of each line? When should ⏎Enter be pressed?
2. What keys move the insertion point without affecting the text?
3. How can you correct typing errors?
4. How do you select a word?
5. What is the purpose of the selection bar?
6. What is the purpose of tool buttons?
7. What is the maximum number of characters that can be used in a filename?
8. Define wordwrap.
9. Why do you have to save files?
10. Can the Spelling feature find all errors? Explain.

EXERCISES

1. Enter the following text. (Your document need not look exactly as it appears here.)
   a. Check the spelling.
   b. Save the file as WD1EX1.
   c. Print the document.

MEMORANDUM

DATE: September 10, 1993

FROM: Lonnie Waters, Social Chairperson

SUBJECT: Fall Picnic

Don't forget to attend this year's Fall Picnic, to be held at the Forest Glade Regional Park on Saturday, September 25, 1993, from 11:00 am to 6:00 pm.

There will be lots of events for the entire family. We'll hold a fishing derby, and there will be races and games for all ages.

You can't beat the price: the food is free to employees and their families. Sign up by the cafeteria.

And don't forget to bring your umbrellas and raincoats, in case it rains like it did at last year's picnic.

2. Enter the text below. (Your document need not look exactly as it appears here.)
   a. Check the spelling.
   b. Save the file as WD1EX2.
   c. Print the document.

September 24, 1993

Mrs. Mildred Adams, Librarian
American Historical Society
1776 Freedom Road
Philadelphia, PA 19100

Dear Mrs. Adams:

I am writing a term paper on quotations of U.S. presidents, focusing on their views of how government should be run. It is easy to find famous quotations for some presidents. Washington, Lincoln, both Roosevelts, and Kennedy are well represented in my research notes.

Could you help me find other noteworthy, if obscure, quotes of the presidents? I've tried Bartlett's "Quotations" and several history textbooks in the school library.

Thank you for your time and patience.

Sincerely,

Donna Lee Light

3. Enter the text below. (Your document need not look exactly as it appears here.)

    a. Check the spelling.

    b. Save the file as WD1EX3.

    c. Print the document.

    Product Initiative Report: Water Saddle

    Al Jenkins, Product Development

    Our department is pleased to announce its latest product invention for advanced testing and market analysis. For years, Cowpokes, Inc., has led the industry in developing innovative products for cattle ranches and rodeos. Recently, our department took a look at dude ranches and found that the demand is growing despite a very low return rate. One of the most frequently mentioned complaints of guests was saddle sores.

    Therefore, we initiated design and preliminary testing of a revolutionary new "water saddle." Like a water bed, its shape conforms to that of the rider, eliminating those bruising pressure points and reducing the tendency to slide about, which causes chafing.

    The water bag is double-sealed in flexible but durable vinyl that simulates the look of cowhide. Preliminary testing indicates more comfort to the rider but a need to reduce wave oscillations. We have some ideas, but this is a subject for advanced testing.

LESSON 2 Formatting Documents

OBJECTIVES

Upon completing the material presented in this lesson, you should understand the following aspects of Microsoft Word:

- [ ] **Using onscreen help**
- [ ] **Opening an existing document**
- [ ] **The default format for printing**
- [ ] **Specifying various format options through commands and through the tool bar, ribbon, and ruler:**
  - **Text alignment**
  - **Centering text**
  - **Line spacing**
  - **Margin settings**
  - **Tab stops**
  - **Line indentation**
  - **Paragraph indentation**
  - **Hanging indent**
  - **Paging**
  - **Page numbering**
- [ ] **Changing font and appearance**

STARTING OFF

Turn on your computer, start Windows, and then launch the Microsoft Word for Windows program as you did in the previous lesson. Insert your data disk in a disk drive. If necessary, maximize the Microsoft Word application window.

USING MICROSOFT WORD ONSCREEN HELP

If you have difficulty understanding or remembering a command or terminology, you can use the extensive onscreen Help system included in Microsoft Word. The onscreen Help feature of Microsoft Word is similar to Help in all Windows applications.

Let's assume right now that you do not remember how to open an existing document.

■   From the Help menu, select Help Index.

Alternative: Press the F1 function key.

▶   *The Microsoft Word Help Index screen appears as shown in Figure 2-1.*

Figure 2-1

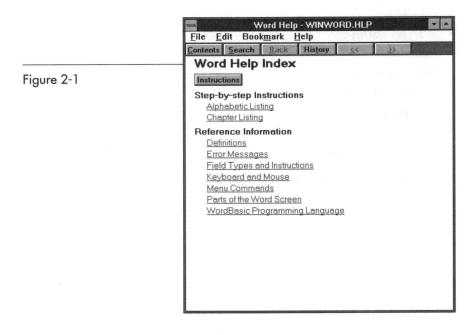

The underlined topics can be selected by clicking on them with a mouse or by pressing ⌨Tab↹ or ⌨⇧Shift+Tab↹ to highlight the topic and then pressing ⌨←Enter.

■　Select "Alphabetic Listing."

▶　*An alphabetic listing of various features appears.*

The list of topics can be scrolled to reveal additional topics. Again, the underlined topics can be selected to reveal further information.

■　Scroll the screen and then select "Opening documents."

▶　*A further listing of related topics appears.*

■　Select "Opening an existing document."

▶　*Step-by-step instructions for opening an existing document are given.*

If you want a paper copy of this information, you can select Print Topic from the File menu in the Word Help window.

■　From the File menu, select Exit to close the Help window.

Alternative:　Press ⌨Alt+F4 or double-click on the control-menu box at the top left edge of the Help window.

You can also do the reverse: Given a command, you can get an explanation of that command.

■　From the File menu, select the Open command.

▶　*The Open dialog box is displayed.*

■　Press the ⌨F1 function key.

▶　*Information about the Open command in the File menu is displayed.*

■　Close the Help window.

■　Click on the Cancel button to exit the Open dialog box.

You can also get help on different regions of the screen, such as a tool button.

■　Press ⌨⇧Shift+F1.

▶　*The mouse pointer turns into a question mark (⮰?).*

■　Point to the open tool button (⬚) and click the left mouse button.

▶　*Again, the Help window describing the Open command is displayed.*

■　Close the Help window.

OPENING AN EXISTING DOCUMENT

Now, let's open a document file. The file to open is MYFILE.DOC, which you saved at the end of the last lesson.

■   From the File menu, select the Open command.

Alternative: Press Ctrl + F12 or click on the open tool button.

▶   *A dialog box appears, as shown in Figure 2-2.*

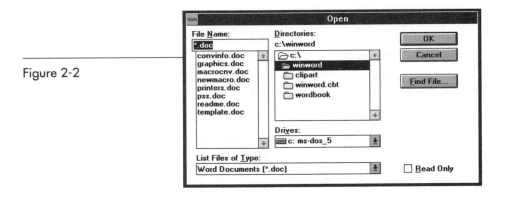

Figure 2-2

The Open dialog box looks similar to the Save As dialog box you saw in the last lesson. It lets you specify the drive, directory, and filename of the document you want retrieved from disk. You will first specify the drive.

NOTE: If your data disk is not in drive A, substitute the appropriate drive name.

■   Click on the down-arrow key at the right end of the Drives list box.

▶   *All available drives are displayed.*

■   Click on a: for drive A.

▶   *The Directories list box displays all directories currently on drive A. If you need to specify the directory, do so by clicking on the directory name.*

The File Name list box on the left displays all the files on the data disk.

■   Click on MYFILE.DOC, and then complete the command by clicking on the OK button or pressing ↵Enter.

▶   *The text from the previous lesson is displayed on the screen.*

DEFAULT FORMAT FOR PRINTING

You might have noticed that when you printed the text at the end of the first lesson, it was printed just about the way it was displayed on the screen. Because the screen display and print formats you used were preset by Microsoft Word (you were using the **default** settings), the document may not have been printed in the format you had in mind. More specifically, the following defaults were used:

Left-aligned, single-spaced

Margins: 1 inch top and bottom, 1.25 inches left and right

Tab stops: every 0.5 inch, left-aligned

These settings can be changed through options in the Format menu and through the tool bar, ribbon, and ruler. If the tool bar, ribbon, or ruler is not displayed on the screen, click on View on the menu bar, and then click on the items you want to display.

TEXT ALIGNMENT

Right now, the text is displayed aligned at the left margin, but not at the right margin. You can change the alignment so text is aligned at the right, centered, or justified. When the text is **justified**, enough blank spaces are inserted in each line so both the left and right margins are aligned.

■ From the Format menu, select Paragraph.

▶ *The Paragraph dialog box is displayed as shown in Figure 2-3.*

Figure 2-3

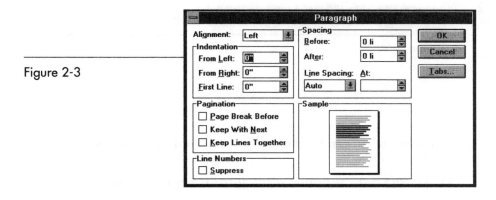

The Alignment text box appears at the top left.

■ Click on the arrow at the right end of the Alignment text box.

▶ *All four options are displayed.*

■ Select Justified and complete the command by clicking on OK or pressing (←Enter).

▶ *The text reflects the change in alignment.*

This could also be done by using the buttons on the ribbon or pressing a combination keystroke. On the ribbon are four buttons for alignment, as shown in Figure 2-4. Right now, the rightmost button, for justified, is selected.

Figure 2-4

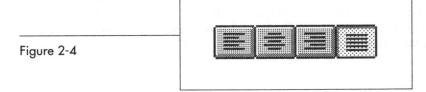

Using combination keystrokes, left alignment can be entered as (Ctrl)+(L), right alignment as (Ctrl)+(R), centered as (Ctrl)+(E), and justified as (Ctrl)+(J).

■ Click on the leftmost button or press (Ctrl)+(L) for left alignment.

▶ *Text is now left-aligned.*

P R A C T I C E   T I M E   2 - 1

1. Select other buttons or press combination keystrokes for alignment and look at the result on the screen.

2. When you are satisfied, set to left alignment.

CENTERING TEXT

There are times when you need text to be **centered**, such as when you enter a title. Let's try it.

■ Position the insertion point at the beginning of the document.

■ Press (←Enter) a couple of times to insert blank lines, and then place the insertion point on the first line.

■ Click on the center button on the ribbon or press Ctrl+E.

▶ *The insertion point jumps to the middle of the line.*

■ Type **LESSON 2 EXAMPLE**.

▶ *The title is centered between the margins.*

N O T E :   To center text that has already been entered, select the text, and then enter the Center command.

LINE SPACING

As mentioned earlier, the default setting for line spacing is single. Actually, the default setting is Auto. Auto not only displays text single-spaced, but also automatically adjusts line height to accommodate various sizes of characters.

■ Position the insertion point anywhere in the text paragraph.

■ From the Format menu, select Paragraph.

▶ *The Paragraph dialog box is displayed.*

You can see the default, Auto, displayed in the Line Spacing list box.

■ Click on the arrow at the right of the Line Spacing list box.

▶ *All available options are displayed.*

■ Select Double.

▶ *The Sample box below shows how the document will be spaced.*

■ Try selecting other options for spacing. Each time look at the Sample box.

■ When you are satisfied, change the spacing back to Auto, the default setting, and then complete the command.

MARGIN SETTINGS

Now, you will look at the margin settings. You can change page margins for selected text or for the entire document. Right now, you will change the margin settings for the entire document.

■ From the Format menu, select Page Setup.

▶ *The Page Setup dialog box is displayed as shown in Figure 2-5.*

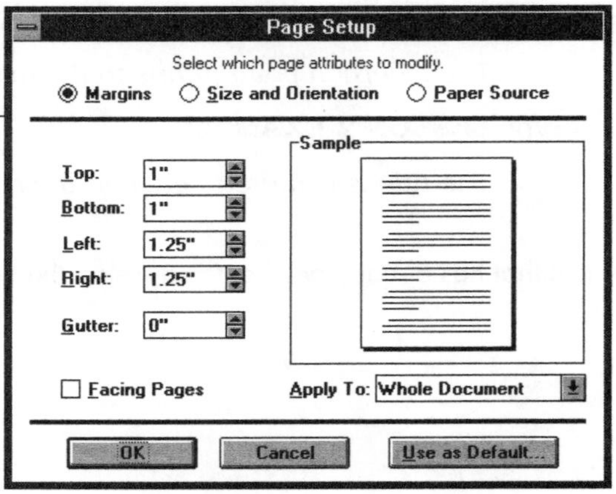

Figure 2-5

■   Make sure the Margins radio button at the top is selected so a dark dot appears.

As you can see, the default settings for top and bottom margins are 1" and for left and right margins are 1.25". To change a margin, just enter a new value for that setting. You will change both the left and right margins to 2".

■   Drag to select the setting for the left margin, and then type **2**.

■   Drag to select the setting for the right margin, and then type **2**.

▶   *Each time, the Sample box on the right displays how text is affected.*

The Apply To text box at the right bottom shows "Whole Document." This means the new margin settings will affect the entire document. Leave the selection as is. If you click the arrow at the right, you will see other options. Right now, the options are Whole Document and This Point Forward. If you were to select This Point Forward, Word would divide the text into a different section starting at the insertion point and would change margins for text in the new section only.

NOTE: If you were to select text and then enter Page Setup, the options in the Apply To text box would be Whole Document or Selected Text.

■   Complete the command by clicking on OK.

▶   *The text reflects the new margin settings.*

THE RULER

Just above the text area is the ruler. You can show either the margin settings or tabs and indent markers on the ruler. If a **[** is displayed to the left of the ruler, the ruler is currently displaying the tabs and indent markers. If you see ▶, the margin markers are displayed.

■   Display the margin settings by clicking on **⌐**, if needed.

▶   *The ruler should look as shown in Figure 2-6.*

Left margin marker —

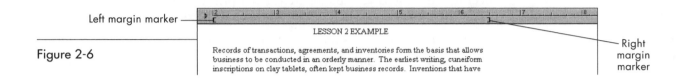

LESSON 2 EXAMPLE

Records of transactions, agreements, and inventories form the basis that allows business to be conducted in an orderly manner. The earliest writing, cuneiform inscriptions on clay tablets, often kept business records. Inventions that have

Right margin marker

Figure 2-6

The ruler starts at 2" at the left edge where the left margin marker is positioned. At the 6½" position, a right margin marker is displayed.

To change the margins for selected text, select the text first, and then drag the margin markers to the desired position. If you drag the margin markers without selecting the text first, you may change the margins for the entire document.

N O T E :   It is possible to divide a document into sections and format each section as you like. A section can be a single paragraph or as long as an entire document. Initially there are no section breaks. Changing margins without selecting text affects the section the insertion point is in.

■   Click on ▶ to the left of the ruler line to display indent markers and tab settings.

▶   *The ruler should look as shown in Figure 2-7.*

Figure 2-7

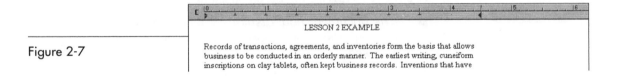

LESSON 2 EXAMPLE

Records of transactions, agreements, and inventories form the basis that allows business to be conducted in an orderly manner. The earliest writing, cuneiform inscriptions on clay tablets, often kept business records. Inventions that have

The ruler line now starts at 0", and markers are shown relative to the left margin setting. In other words, the 0" position is at the left margin, which is 2" from the left edge of the paper.

At the 0" position, you see the **left indent marker** (bottom triangle) and the ***first-line indent marker*** (top triangle). At the 4.5" position, you see the **right indent marker** (full triangle). The left indent marker tells how much the text is to be indented relative to the left margin. The right indent marker tells the line width. The first-line indent marker is explained later. The ruler also shows default tab stops at every half-inch interval between the two markers.

TABS AND NONPRINTING CHARACTERS

Tab settings, or stops, determine the position of the insertion point each time the Tab⇥ key is pressed. When you press Tab⇥, a ***nonprinting character*** is inserted in the document. Hence, if you want to remove the effect of pressing Tab⇥, you delete the nonprinting character. To make this task easier, you can display nonprinting characters.

■ From the Tools menu, select Options.

▶ *The Options dialog box appears as shown in Figure 2-8.*

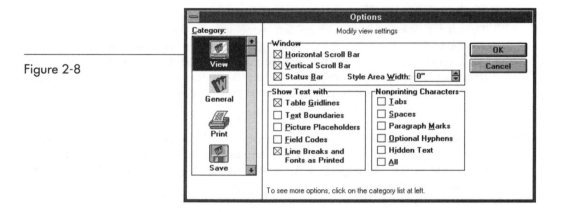

Figure 2-8

■ In the Nonprinting Characters box, select All so an X appears in the check box, and then complete the command.

Alternative: Press the last button on the ribbon (¶).

▶ *The document now displays ¶ wherever you pressed ←Enter. Also, dots appear wherever the spacebar was pressed.*

■ Position the insertion point at the end of the document, and then press ←Enter to position the insertion point at the beginning of a new line.

■ Press Tab⇥.

▶ *The nonprinting character (→) appears.*

To hide the nonprinting characters, follow the exact same steps you used to display them: Choose Options from the Tools menu and then click on All (so that the X disappears), or press the button on the ribbon.

P R A C T I C E   T I M E   2 - 2

Hide the nonprinting characters.

SETTING TABS

By default, tab stops are set to every half inch, starting at the left margin. You can insert or delete custom tabs. To add custom tab stops, you select the paragraph(s) you want affected by the new tab stops and then set the tab stops. You can set tabs by using the ruler or by choosing the Tabs command from the Format menu. If you do not make a text selection first, tab stops are set for the paragraph that contains the insertion point. When you set a custom tab stop, Word clears all default tab stops to the left of the custom tab stop.

N O T E :   Word stores tab settings in the paragraph mark at the end of each paragraph. If you delete a paragraph mark, not only does the text become part of the following paragraph, but you also delete the tab settings for that text.

■   From the Forma<u>t</u> menu, select <u>T</u>abs.

▶   *The Tabs dialog box, as shown in Figure 2-9, is displayed.*

Figure 2-9

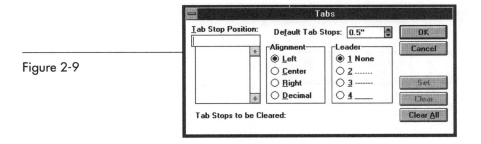

To set a tab, type the location in the Tab Stop Position text box, and then click the Set button. To clear a tab, click on the tab setting in the Tab Stop Position list box, and then click the Clear button. To clear all tab settings, click the Clear All button.

The Alignment selection box lets you indicate the kind of tab setting. The effects of these types of tab settings are discussed in the next lesson. The Leader selection box is not discussed here.

Right now you will set custom tab stops at columns 1" and 2".
Remember, tab settings are indicated relative to the left margin.

■ With the insertion bar in the Tab Stop Position text box, type **1**
and then select Set.

▶ *1" appears in the Tab Stop Position list box.*

■ Now change the entry in the Tab Stop Position text box to 2,
and then select Set.

▶ *2" appears in the Tab Stop Position list box.*

■ Complete the command.

▶ *The ruler displays custom tab stops at 1" and 2" positions,*
and all default tab stops to the left are cleared.

You will now delete the tab stop at 2".

■ From the Format menu, select Tabs to display the Tabs dialog
box.

■ Select 2" in the Tab Stop Position list box.

■ Select Clear and then complete the command.

▶ *The custom tab stop at 2" is cleared.*

You can also insert, remove, and move tab stops using the ribbon and ruler.
On the ribbon toward the right are four buttons with arrows as shown in
Figure 2-10. These indicate different types of tab stops. All you need to do to
set a tab is to select the style of tab stop you want on the ribbon and then
click on the ruler where you want the tab stop.

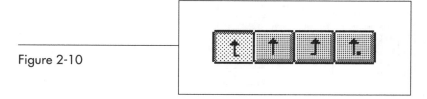

Figure 2-10

Of the four tab buttons displayed on the ribbon, the leftmost displays
the same marker as the current custom tab. That is the left tab button.
Others are center tab, right tab, and decimal tab, and they are explained in
the next lesson.

■ Click on the left tab button, if necessary, and then click at the
2" position on the ruler.

▶ *A custom left tab stop is inserted.*

To get rid of any unwanted tab, drag the tab marker off the ruler.

■ Drag the custom tab stop at 2" off the ruler.

▶ *The custom tab stop at 2" is cleared.*

PRACTICE TIME 2-3

1. Set tab stops at various positions using both the Format menu and the ruler.

2. When you are satisfied, clear all custom tab stops so the default settings remain in effect.

LINE INDENTATION

Suppose you want to indent the first line of a paragraph by ½". One way you can do this is to make sure there is a tab stop at ½" and then press [Tab↹] at the beginning of each paragraph. There is also another way. You can set the first-line indent to 0.5". The first-line indent marker initially is at the same position as the left indent marker. Once the first-line indent marker is positioned, Word will indent the first line of each paragraph automatically.

- Position the insertion point at the end of the document.

- Press [←Enter] twice to insert a blank line.

- From the Format menu, select Paragraph.

  ▶ *The Paragraph dialog box is displayed.*

Under Indentation, the last text box is for the First Line indentation.

- Drag to select the number in First Line and type **0.5**.

- Complete the command.

  ▶ *The insertion point moves to the 0.5" position. Also, notice the position of the first-line indent marker on the ruler.*

PRACTICE TIME 2-4

1. Enter the following text:

   When a computer is instructed to do a job, it handles the task in a very special way. It accepts the information. It stores the information until the information is ready to be used. It processes the information. Then it gives out the processed information.

2. Save the file as FILE1.DOC. Enter whatever summary information you think appropriate.

Another way you could have set the first-line indentation is to drag the first-line indent marker on the ruler to the desired position. Right now, you will use the ruler to return the first-line indent marker to the 0" position.

■   Drag the first-line indent marker to the 0" position.

▶   *The insertion point moves back to the 0" position.*

PARAGRAPH INDENTATION

Sometimes you need to indent a whole paragraph for emphasis, such as when you are quoting from another source. What you want to do is change the value of the left margin for a little while. You could change the left and right margins for the selected text, but there is another way.

■   Position the insertion point at the end of the document.

■   Press (←Enter) twice to insert a blank line.

■   Drag the left indent marker to the ½" position. Remember, the left indent marker is the bottom triangle. When you drag the left indent marker, the first-line indent marker moves with it.

▶   *The insertion point moves to the ½" position.*

■   Type the following:

The concept behind word processing is a fascinating one. The typewriter has become archaic, stricken by a single technological blow. The concepts of training and productivity have changed, too. The more productive worker is the one who can insert text changes, make corrections, move blocks of text, and otherwise process text rewrites efficiently.

■   Press (←Enter).

▶   *Your screen should look similar to Figure 2-11.*

■   Save the file again, using the same name.

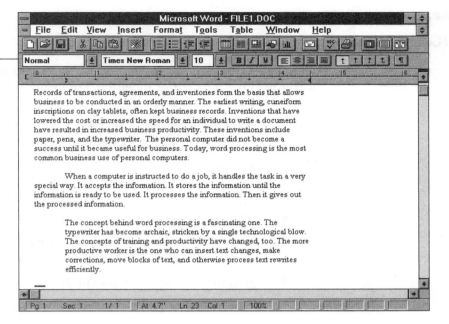

Figure 2-11

P R A C T I C E   T I M E   2 - 5

1. Delete the first and third paragraphs.

2. Place the insertion point somewhere in the remaining paragraph.

3. Change both left and right margins to 3" (3" and 5½" positions, respectively).

4. Set the first-line indent to 0".

5. Insert ←Enter and numbers so the paragraph looks similar to Figure 2-12. (You press Tab⇆ after each number.)

6. Save the file as FILE2.DOC.

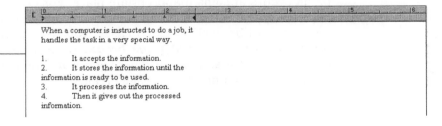

Figure 2-12

HANGING INDENT

When you number a sentence, and it runs on to more than one line, the "turnover" lines look better indented. For example, item 2 in the list should look like this:

> 2. It stores the information until the
>   information is ready to be used.

When a sentence or item is in this format, it is said to be in **hanging indent** format. A hanging indent indents all but the first line of the paragraph.

- ■ Select all four numbered sentences.

- ■ Drag the left indent marker (along with the first-line indent marker) to the ½" position.

- ■ Drag just the first-line indent marker to the 0" position.

> ▶ *The text should look similar to Figure 2-13.*

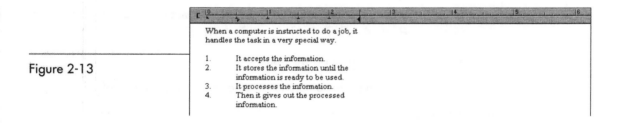

Figure 2-13

PAGING

When you have a long, multiple-page document, Microsoft Word shows you where the printer will advance to a new page. This is known as a **soft page break** and is shown as a horizontal dotted line on the screen.

As you look over the document, however, you may find that a soft page break occurs at some inappropriate place. For example, you do not want a page break to occur in the middle of a table, or you may want an item to be on a page all by itself. In such cases, you need to manually enter a page break, known as a **hard page break**. A hard page break is entered by positioning the insertion bar where you want the page break to occur and inserting the command for a page break.

■   Open FILE1.DOC.

■   Place the insertion point at the end of the first paragraph.

■   From the <u>I</u>nsert menu, select <u>B</u>reak. Then select OK.

Alternative: Press Ctrl + ←Enter.

▶   *A line is inserted after the first paragraph, as shown in Figure 2-14.*

Figure 2-14

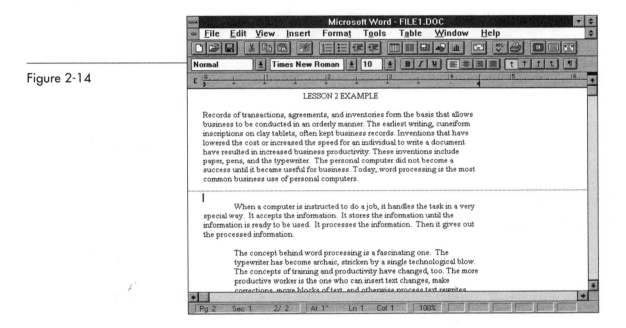

■   From the <u>F</u>ile menu, select Print Pre<u>v</u>iew.

▶   *The first page of the document is displayed. It only shows the first paragraph.*

■   Click on the Two P<u>a</u>ges button at the top.

▶   *Two pages are displayed as shown in Figure 2-15.*

NOTE: From this preview screen, you can print the document by clicking on the <u>P</u>rint button.

■   Click on Close.

Should you decide that you do not want the hard page break after all, position the insertion point just after the break and press ←Backspace.

Figure 2-15

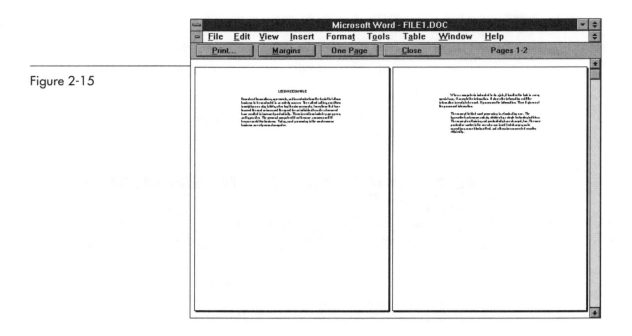

PAGE NUMBERING

When you are creating a multiple-page document, you may want to print the page number on each page.

◼ Position the insertion point anywhere in the first page of the text.

◼ From the Insert menu, select Page Numbers.

▶ *The Page Numbers dialog box is displayed, as shown in Figure 2-16.*

Figure 2-16

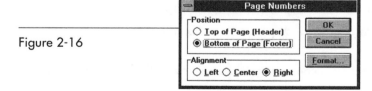

You can insert the page number at the top or the bottom of the paper. The bottom is the default selection. Also, the number can appear at the left, center, or right. Right is the default selection. You will use the default settings.

NOTE: Through the Format option, you can specify the type of numbers to be Arabic numerals (1, 2, 3), lowercase Roman numerals (i, ii, iii), or uppercase Roman numerals (I, II, III). You can also specify the starting number for paging.

■ Complete the command.

Page numbers can be inserted using the Footer command or through the Page Numbers command. When you use the Page Numbers command, however, Word does not print a page number on the first page of the document. To print the page number on the first page, do the following:

■ From the View menu, select Header/Footer.

■ Clear the Different First Page check box by clicking on it.

▶ *X disappears from the check box.*

■ Complete the command.

■ Click Close to close the Header/Footer dialog box.

PRACTICE TIME 2 - 6

1. Preview or print the text to look at the page numbering.

2. Delete the hard page break.

CHANGING FONT

The appearance of characters on your screen and printout is determined by three things collectively called the **font:** the typeface, the size, and the appearance.

- The **typeface** is the graphic design of the characters and is given a name such as Courier, Helvetica, or Times Roman. The typeface is often referred to as the font.

- The size of the character will depend on the type of font. If the font you choose is **proportionally spaced** (different widths for different letters), the size is given in **points**, or the height of a capital letter in 72nds of an inch. Typical fonts are 10- or 12-point fonts, with 10 being the smaller size. If the font you choose is **monospaced** (each letter requires the same amount of space), the size is indicated in **characters per inch**, or **cpi**. Again, the typical font sizes are 10 cpi or 12 cpi, with 12 cpi being the smaller size.

- The appearance includes regular, bold, italic, and underline. These styles can be used alone or in any combination.

You can select an appropriate font for display and printing the document. The style can be varied to emphasize certain information. The font and size will affect how much text can fit on one page of the document.

To change a text font, you select the text you want to change or position the insertion point where you want to begin typing characters with the new font. If you want to change the default font selection, the insertion point can be anywhere. When you change the default setting, the entire document will use the font specified.

■   Select a section of the text.

■   From the Format menu, choose Character.

▶   *The Character dialog box is displayed, as shown in Figure 2-17.*

Figure 2-17

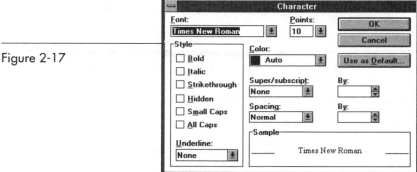

■   Click on the down arrow next to the Font list box.

▶   *All font options are displayed.*

■   Select a font style.

▶   *The Sample box displays the font selected.*

NOTE: If you want to change the default font selection, select the Use as Default button.

■   Complete the command.

▶   *The selected text changes to the font specified.*

You can also change the font by using the ribbon or by pressing a combination keystroke. (You cannot change the default font selection this way.)

■   Click on the down arrow next to the second box from the left on the ribbon, or press Ctrl+F.

▶   *Font options are displayed.*

■   Click the font name you want.

Depending on the font selected, you will have different point sizes to choose from. Size selection is very similar to the font selection. You can specify size by using the Character command from the Format menu or by choosing the size box on the ribbon. You can also press Ctrl+P. Try this on your own.

P R A C T I C E   T I M E   2 - 7

Try various fonts and sizes, and study the effects.

CHANGING APPEARANCE

You can change the appearance of characters either as you type the text or after it has been typed. As mentioned earlier, appearance includes bold, underline, and italic.

•   To change appearance while entering text, position the insertion point where you plan to enter text, give the command to change appearance, type the text, and then give the command again to return to normal appearance.

•   To change the appearance of text already typed, select the desired text and then give the command to change the appearance.

Again, commands can be given using the Character command in the Format menu or using the ribbon buttons. The ribbon has three buttons, as shown in Figure 2-18, for bold, italic, and underline.

Figure 2-18

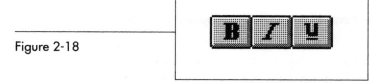

■   Position the insertion point at the end of the document.

■   Press ←Enter a couple of times to insert a blank line.

■   Click the italic button or press Ctrl+I.

■   Type the following:

This text is being entered in italics.

▶   *The text appears in italics on the screen.*

■   Click the italic button again to return to normal characters.

Now, assume you want the title to appear in bold characters. Because the title has been typed already, you have to select the text of the title and then give the Bold command.

■   Drag the mouse to select the text of the title.

■   Click the bold button or press ⌈Ctrl⌉+⌈B⌉.

▶   *The title is now in bold characters.*

■   Click elsewhere to deselect the text.

PRACTICE   TIME   2 - 8

Try the underline feature on your own. The combination keystroke for underline is ⌈Ctrl⌉+⌈U⌉.

ENDING LESSON 2

This is the end of Lesson 2. Exit Microsoft Word and quit Windows as explained in Lesson 1. There is no need to save changes you made to your files.

SUMMARY

In this lesson, many of the terms and concepts that are related to how text appears on the printout are introduced.

☐   **The default values set by the Microsoft Word program dictate how a document appears on the screen and on printouts. These values can be changed by using either the menu commands or the tool bar, ribbon, and ruler.**

☐   **First-line indentation is when the first line of a paragraph is indented. To do this, set a tab at the appropriate position and use the ⌈Tab↹⌉ key or set the first-line indent marker to the desired position.**

☐   **To change the font or appearance of text, you either (1) give the command, type text, and enter the command again, or (2) select the text and then give the command to change appearance.**

KEY TERMS

centered	hard page break	proportionally spaced
characters per inch (cpi)	justified	characters
default	left indent marker	right indent marker
first-line indent marker	monospaced characters	soft page break
font	nonprinting characters	tabs
hanging indent	points	typeface

COMMAND SUMMARY

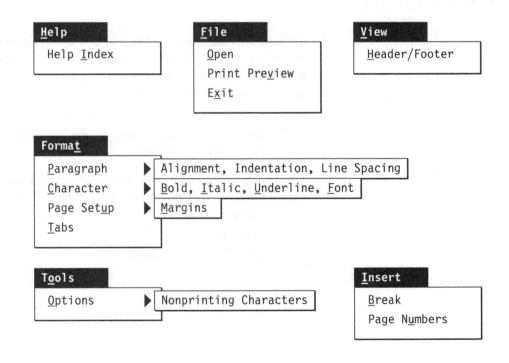

R E V I E W   Q U E S T I O N S

1. What is the difference between a soft return and a hard return and between a soft page break and a hard page break?

2. If you do not specify the left and right margins, what values are used?

3. What does text alignment mean? What are the options?

4. What does hanging indent mean? What commands do you give to use hanging indent?

5. How do you indent an entire paragraph?

6. How do you underline characters? How do you make characters bold?

7. What can you do with the ruler?

8. Give examples of formats you can change using the ribbon.

9. How do you set tabs using the Tabs command; using the ruler?

10. Give the keystrokes needed to make page numbers appear at the top right corner of each page.

E X E R C I S E S

1. Retrieve the letter saved in the previous lesson as WD1EX2. Make the following changes, get a printout, and save the file as WD2EX1.
   a. Center the date on the first line.
   b. Make sure the text is left-aligned.
   c. Indent all text by 3.5" starting just before "Sincerely."
   d. Remove the quotation marks from the book title "Quotations." Underline the title instead.

2. Enter the following text. (Your text need not look exactly as it appears here. However, you should set new tabs before entering the recipe.)
   a. Check the spelling.
   b. Get a printout.
   c. Save the file on the disk as WD2EX2.

Dear Jill:

I've just come across the most wonderful spaghetti sauce recipe.

1 pound	Italian hot sausage
1 can (4 ounces)	sliced mushrooms, drained
3/4 cup	shredded carrots
1	medium onion, grated
1/2 cup	chopped parsley
1 pound	ground beef
1 can (28 ounces)	Italian style tomatoes
2 cans (6 ounces)	tomato paste
1 cup	dry red wine
1	bay leaf
2 teaspoons	salt
1 teaspoon	basil leaves
1/4 teaspoon	pepper
1 pound	spaghetti

In a large pan, cook sausage in 1/4 cup water for 10 minutes, tightly covered, stirring occasionally. Remove sausage. In that pan, saute mushrooms, carrot, onion, celery, and parsley in sausage drippings until crisp and tender. Remove. Add beef. Cook, stirring frequently, until lightly browned. Remove any excess fat. Return sausage and vegetables to pan. Add tomatoes, tomato paste, wine, bay leaf, salt, basil, and pepper. Cover and simmer 30 minutes. Uncover and simmer 2 hours, stirring occasionally. Remove bay leaf. Meanwhile, cook spaghetti according to directions on package. Serve with grated Parmesan cheese.

Sounds great, doesn't it? It tastes <u>delicious</u>.

Your friend,

Jackie

3. Enter the following text. (Your text need not look exactly as it appears here.)
    a. Check the spelling.
    b. Get a printout.
    c. Save the file on the disk as WD2EX3.

IDEA PROCESSING

The phrases "word processing" and "data processing" are becoming more and more prevalent in common language. In the mid-1970s, who owned a word processor? What these phrases actually refer to is idea processing. With the recent growth in computer technology available to consumers, idea processing has evolved rapidly.

In many ways, idea processing has opened previously inaccessible avenues for businesses and individuals:

*   Point-of-entry data terminals in a store can immediately register sales and provide data for efficient inventory and management decisions.

*   Financial models can show a board of directors the cold figures, which, in past times, were only available <u>after</u> the decision making had taken place.

*   Form letters no longer need to be individually typed, using so much secretarial time.

*   Because businesses and individuals can obtain immediate access to a variety of data sets over phone lines, the possibilities for idea processing seem limited by the mind only.

And the mind is indeed the crucial element in idea processing. For, without an accurate financial model, the best available data are worthless; without proper thought, inventory and management decisions can be detrimental to the company's well-being; without a specific and detailed method for <u>how</u> data are to be processed, access to timely data is worthless.

3 Advanced Editing Features

O B J E C T I V E S

Upon completing the material presented in this lesson, you should understand the following aspects of Microsoft Word:

- ☐ **Opening multiple documents**

- ☐ **Switching between document windows**

- ☐ **Copying selected text from one word processing file to another**

- ☐ **Entering text right-aligned and decimal-aligned**

- ☐ **Including current date**

- ☐ **Specifying tab alignment**

- ☐ **Finding a particular word or combination of words in a text**

- ☐ **Replacing a particular word or combination of words in a text with a specified word or combination of words**

- ☐ **Using merge**

STARTING OFF

Turn on your computer, start Windows, and then launch the Microsoft Word for Windows program as you did in previous lessons. Insert your data disk in the disk drive. If necessary, maximize the Microsoft Word application window.

OPENING MULTIPLE FILES

As was mentioned in Lesson 1, the workspace for Windows can contain up to nine documents, if your computer has enough available memory. You will open two files: MYFILE and FILE1 from your data disk.

P R A C T I C E   T I M E   3 - 1

1. Open MYFILE from your data disk.

2. Open FILE1 from your data disk.

You can only see the contents of FILE1 on the screen right now.

Switching Between Windows

You can switch between document windows through the Window menu.

■   Click on Window in the menu bar.

▶   *The pull-down menu appears, as shown in Figure 3-1.*

Figure 3-1

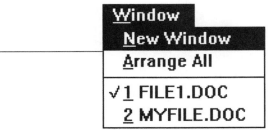

The two documents appear as command options. Select the document you want to be the ***active window***. The active document is the one you can work with. In the Window menu, the active file has a checkmark in front of it.

■   Select 2.

▶   *The document MYFILE is made active.*

P R A C T I C E   T I M E   3 - 2

Make the document FILE1 active.

There are also other ways to switch the active window.

Arranging Windows

■   From the <u>W</u>indow menu, select the <u>A</u>rrange All command.

▶   *Two document windows appear in the Microsoft Word workspace as shown in Figure 3-2.*

Figure 3-2

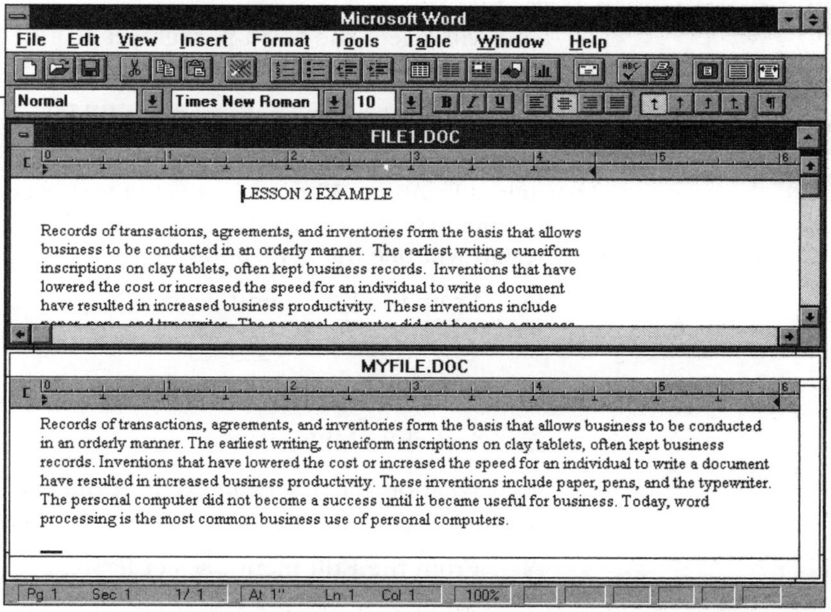

You can easily see that two document windows are now open in the workspace. The active window is the one in which the insertion point appears and that has a darker title bar.

■   Click anywhere in the other document window.

▶   *The MYFILE document is now the active window.*

■   Maximize the MYFILE document window.

P R A C T I C E   T I M E   3 - 3

1. Arrange the windows, and then make FILE1 the active window.

2. Maximize the FILE1 window.

MOVING SELECTED TEXT BETWEEN DOCUMENTS

Sometimes you need to take a passage of text out of one document and insert it into another. In Microsoft Word, moving selected text between two documents is no different from moving it within a document. You cut or copy selected text onto the Clipboard, and then you paste the text where you want it.

You will select the third paragraph of FILE1 so it can be included in MYFILE.

■   Select the third paragraph of FILE1.

The selected text can be cut or copied. When you cut, the text is no longer in the original location. When the selected text is copied, however, the original stays intact. Because you do not want to remove this paragraph from FILE1, you will use the copy option.

■   From the Edit menu, select Copy.

Alternative: Press Ctrl+C.

▶   *The selected text is copied onto the Clipboard.*

■   Switch to MYFILE.

■   Position the insertion point at the end of the document. Press ←Enter a couple of times to insert a blank line.

■   From the Edit menu, select Paste.

Alternative: Press ⇧Shift+V.

▶   *The selected text is inserted as shown in Figure 3-3.*

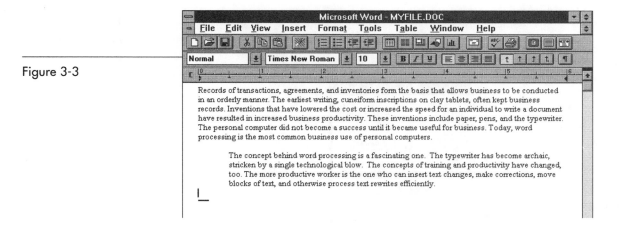

Figure 3-3

P R A C T I C E   T I M E   3 - 4

1. Copy the first paragraph from MYFILE to a new document.

   Hint: Copy, open a new document, and then paste.

2. Arrange all document windows.

3. Close all files. There is no need to save changes.

OPENING A NEW DOCUMENT

A document ***template*** is a special document you can use as a pattern to create other documents of the same type. For example, you can create a document template for letters that makes it easy to produce letters that follow the same format. When you use a template, you no longer have to start from scratch each time you create a document. Tasks such as setting the margins, choosing a font, and creating headers and footers have already been taken care of.

Microsoft Word comes with a several predefined templates for the most common types of documents. By default, new documents are based on a file called NORMAL.DOT—the NORMAL template.

Every Word document is based on a document template. In fact, it's impossible to create a new document that is not based on a template. If you don't select a template when you create a new document, Word bases the new document on the NORMAL template.

■   From the File menu, select New.

▶   *The New dialog box appears as shown in Figure 3-4.*

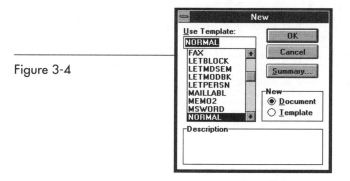

Figure 3-4

You can see that NORMAL has already been selected for use and appears in the Use Template text box.

■   Complete the command.

▶   *A document window appears.*

ENTERING TEXT FLUSH RIGHT

Most of the time, you enter text starting at the left margin; other than line indentation, you want your lines to be ***left-aligned***, or to line up at the left margin. If you also want the text to be aligned at the right margin, you turn the alignment to justified. There are times, however, when you want the text to be ***right-aligned*** without any regard to the left margin. An example might be when you are entering the date at the beginning of a letter.

■   From the Format menu, select Paragraph. Then set the Alignment to Right and complete the command.

Alternative: Click on the right alignment button in the ribbon (▤).

▶   *The insertion point moves to the right margin.*

■   Type **December 14, 1993** and press ⏎Enter.

▶   *The text is entered right-aligned (even with the right margin).*

P R A C T I C E   T I M E   3 - 5

Set the alignment to Left.

INCLUDING THE CURRENT DATE

Your PC keeps track of time when the PC is on. If you do not have a battery-operated clock (which stays on when the computer is turned off), you have the option to enter the current date and time when you start up the computer. Nevertheless, there is an internal clock that keeps time and date information. You can have the Microsoft Word program insert the current date (as kept by the internal clock) into the document.

■   From the Insert menu, select Date and Time.

▶   *The Date and Time dialog box appears as shown in Figure 3-5.*

Figure 3-5

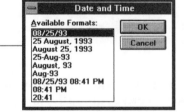

The Available Formats box displays all available formats.

■   Click on the format you want, such as the third one down, and complete the command.

▶   *The current date is inserted at the insertion point, in the format you selected.*

Word inserts the date or time as a field code, which it updates at printing. If you want, you can update as you work by positioning the insertion point in the date or time and pressing the Update Field key ([F9]). If you don't want the date or time to be updated at all, position the insertion point and press the Unlink Field key ([Ctrl]+[⇧Shift]+[F9]).

PRACTICE TIME 3-6

1. Close the current document window without saving.

2. Start a new document and enter the partial letter given below. The opening address and date are to be entered flush right.

1728 Forest Road
Takoma Park, Maryland
<current date>

Mr. Gary Bradshaw
Computer Parts Shop
1234 Byte Street
Golden, Colorado 81234

Dear Mr. Bradshaw:

Please accept my orders for the following items:

3. Save the text on your data disk as LETTER1.

TAB ALIGNMENT

In the letter you started in the previous Practice Time, the next step is to specify the items you want to order, quantity, and price, as shown below:

50	**boxes of diskettes @14.75**	**$737.50**
5	**printer ribbons @11.95**	**59.75**
1	**diskette container @9.95**	**9.95**

The first column is typed right-aligned (at a specific position, +1" in this case), the second column is typed left-aligned (at another specific position, +1.5" in this case), and the third column needs to be aligned at the decimal point (at position +5" in this case). You can set the tabs so this type of data entry is simple.

- Make sure the insertion point is at the bottom of the letter. (There should be at least one blank line after the end of the text.)

- From the Format menu, select Tabs.

  ▶ *The Tabs dialog box is displayed.*

You will set tabs at +1", +1.5", and +5". However, at +1", you want to specify right alignment; at +1.5", left alignment; and at +5", decimal alignment.

■ Click on Right in the Alignment radio box, type **1** in the Tab Stop Position text box, and then click on Set.

■ Click on Left in the Alignment radio box, type **1.5** in the Tab Stop Position text box, and then click on Set.

■ Click on Decimal in the Alignment radio box, type **5** in the Tab Stop Position box, and then click on Set.

■ Complete the command.

▶ *The ruler appears as shown in Figure 3-6.*

Figure 3-6

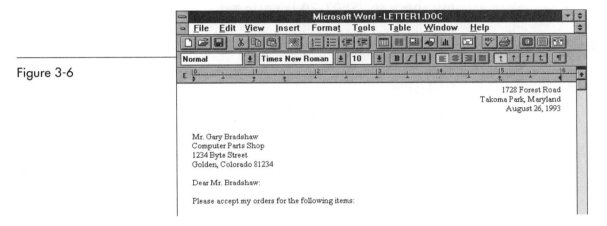

NOTE: You could have set these tabs by dragging the appropriate tab icon from the ribbon to the ruler. As mentioned earlier, the four tab icons in the ribbon are left, center, right, and decimal alignment tabs.

■ Press Tab↹.

▶ *The insertion point jumps to the first tab setting.*

■ Type **50**

▶ *The entry is made flush right at position +1".*

■ Press Tab↹.

▶ *The insertion point jumps to position +1.5".*

■ Type **boxes of diskettes @14.75**

▶ *The entry is made flush left at position +1.5".*

■ Press Tab↹.

▶ *The insertion point jumps to position +5".*

■ Type **$737.50**

▶ *The entry is made with the decimal point at position +5".*

■ Press ↵Enter.

P R A C T I C E   T I M E   3 - 7

1. Type in the next two items.

2. Insert a blank line after the third item.

3. Reset the tabs so they appear every 0.5". (Hint: Select Clear All in the Tabs dialog box or drag all custom tabs off the ruler.)

4. Enter the rest of the letter.

   My check for $807.20 is enclosed.

   Sincerely,

   \<your name\>

   Enclosure

5. Save the text again using the same filename.

6. Close the file LETTER1.

FINDING TEXT

There are times when you need to *find* text—move the insertion point to a specific word that you know is somewhere in the document. Microsoft Word has a command to help you do just that. You can search from the insertion point either forward or backward in a document.

■　Open MYFILE from your data disk.

■　Place the insertion point at the beginning of the document so you can do a "down" search.

Pretend this is a long document on record management and you need to find the word "cuneiform" because you have additional information you want to insert.

■　From the Edit menu, select Find.

▶　*The Find dialog box appears as shown in Figure 3-7.*

In the Find What box, you need to enter the text you want to find. You can type up to 255 characters in the Find What box. Text scrolls horizontally in the box as you type.

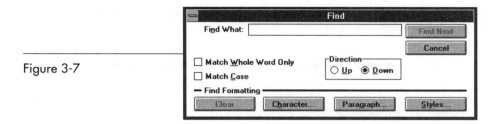

Figure 3-7

The Direction radio box shows that you are set for a down search, which means the search is made "down" the document from the current position of the insertion point.

If you do not select Match Whole Word Only, Word will also find text that is part of another word. For example, if you are searching for the last name Thorn, Word will locate Thornapple as well. If you select Match Whole Word Only, Word will find only separate, whole words, not characters embedded within other words.

If you do not select Match Case, the search is not case-sensitive, which means the text is matched with both upper- and lowercase occurrences within the document. If you select Match Case, however, the search is case-sensitive, and Microsoft Word looks for an exact match.

■   In the Find What box, type **cuneiform**, and then click on Find Next.

▶   *The first occurrence of the word "cuneiform" is highlighted.*

■   Click on Cancel to close the Find dialog box.

PRACTICE TIME 3-8

Find all occurrences of the word "productivity" in MYFILE.

N O T E :   When you initiate the search, the word "cuneiform" still appears in the Find What box. Just type "productivity." It will replace the previous entry.

REPLACING WORDS

In the course of editing a document, sometimes you want to look for a particular word that needs to be replaced. For example, assume you have written a lengthy report on a client only to find out that there has been a change in the client's company name. Rather than searching through the entire document visually, looking for each occurrence of the company name and replacing the name, you'd like the Microsoft Word program to find and ***replace*** the name for you.

PRACTICE TIME 3-9

1. Open a new document.

2. Enter the following text and then save the file as LETTER2.

November 30, 1993

Mr. John Smith
Personnel Office
Republic Engineering
3570 Fruitland Avenue
Maywood, OR 97119

Dear Mr. Smith:

This is a letter of application for the draftsperson position advertised by Republic Engineering. As you will notice in the enclosed resume, my background is just what Republic Engineering is looking for.

Please notice also that I have twice been selected as employee of the month in my current job. Republic Engineering is surely interested in my loyal attitude toward my employer.

I look forward to hearing from you concerning an interview date and time. In the meanwhile, could you provide me with some information concerning the medical and retirement benefits available to Republic Engineering employees?

Thank you.

Sincerely,

Michael Gregory

Encl.

You just found out that Mr. John Smith is no longer with Republic Engineering. The letter has to be sent to Mr. John Matthews.

- ▓ Place the insertion point at the beginning of the letter.

- ▓ From the Edit menu, select Replace.

  - ▶ *The Replace dialog box, as shown in Figure 3-8, is displayed.*

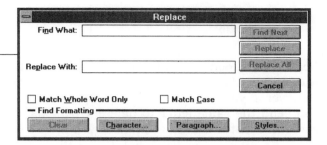

Figure 3-8

First you need to specify the character string you want to find.

■ With the insertion point in the Find What text box, type **Smith** (do not press ⎰←Enter⎱).

Now, you need to specify what to replace Smith with.

■ Position the insertion point in the Replace With text box.

■ Type **Matthews**.

As you did with the Find command earlier, you need to indicate whether or not you want to match whole words only and whether you want to do a case-sensitive search. You will leave these unselected.

You have an option of clicking the Find Next button or the Replace All button. If you click the Replace All button, you can have all occurrences of Smith replaced with Matthews without having to approve each one. With the Find Next button, Word will pause after finding each occurrence.

■ Click on the Find Next button to start the search.

▶ *The first occurrence of Smith is highlighted.*

■ Click on the Replace button.

▶ *Smith is replaced with Matthews, and the next occurrence of Smith is found.*

■ Keep confirming the replacement until all occurrences of Smith have been replaced by Matthews. You will know this is done when no more text is selected.

P R A C T I C E   T I M E   3 - 1 0

1. Replace all occurrences of Republic Engineering with Conway Architects without confirming them individually.

2. Save the letter as LETTER3.

3. Close all documents.

MERGE

Replace is a good command to use if you are just substituting one phrase with another (or several phrases with several other phrases) one time only. However, if you need to do this a multiple number of times, such as when you send the same letter to different persons, you should use the Merge command instead.

The letter or the document itself, called the ***main document***, needs to be modified to contain the codes where names and addresses should be inserted. Names and addresses, or whatever other information will be merged into the main document, are entered in a separate file referred to as the ***data file***. The command then ***merges*** the two files to create as many merged documents as there are sets of information in the data file, with the proper information inserted at indicated positions.

These two files can be created in whatever order you want. What matters is that the order in which information is supplied in the data file matches up with the codes in the main document. Right now, you will create the data file first and then create the main document.

Here is the letter you want to send out:

July 20, 1993

Sam Sherman
3983 West Blvd.
Los Angeles, CA 90016

Dear **Sam**:

If you need $2,000 worth of equipment right away, it's a serious matter. And borrowing money to make the purchase is not always easy. But because you, **Sam**, have a good credit rating with us, you are now preapproved for a $2,000 credit limit.

If you are interested, give us a call and one of our sales people will visit you in your fair city of **Los Angeles** right away. Also, if you need more than a $2,000 credit limit, **Sam**, please let us know. We'll go out of our way to help you any way we can.

Sincerely,

In the letter, all text that is displayed in bold characters is personalizing information. The idea is to create as many copies of this letter as you have names and addresses in the data file, with all of the letters personalized. This means that, within the letter, you need to specify where to insert first name, address, city, and so forth.

Data File

You will use the Print Merge command to create the data file. The data you enter is organized into data records in a table. The field names appear in the first row of cells, the **header record**, and act as column headings for the address information.

N O T E :   All information related to a person appears in a row and is referred to as a **record**. Each record contains **fields**: a field that contains first name, a field that contains last name, a field that contains street address, and so on. All records in a data file must contain the same fields, listed in the same order.

The first step in creating a new data file is to decide which information you want to vary in each version of the merged document. Once you determine the fields, you need to give them field names. A field name can be up to 32 characters. You can use letters, numbers, and underscore characters, but not spaces. The following fields (field names) are needed for this example:

Field 1	FirstName
Field 2	LastName
Field 3	Company
Field 4	StreetAddress
Field 5	City
Field 6	State
Field 7	ZipCode

The first record contains Kay Gray of Buttons & Banners. The address is P.O. Box 2110, Incline Village, NV 89450.

■ From the File menu, select New.

▶ *The New dialog box appears.*

■ Click on OK or press (←Enter).

■ From the File menu, select Print Merge.

▶ *The Print Merge Setup dialog box appears as shown in Figure 3-9.*

■ Click on Attach Data File.

▶ *The Attach Data File dialog box is displayed.*

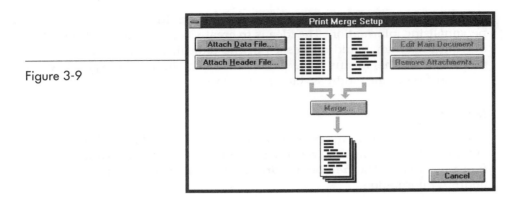

Figure 3-9

■ Click on Create Data File.

▶ *The Create Data File dialog box is displayed.*

■ In the Field Name text box, type the name of the first field, **FirstName**, and then click on Add.

▶ *The field FirstName appears in the list box.*

■ Type the second field, **LastName**, and click Add.

▶ *The field is added to the list.*

■ Type and add the rest of the fields: **Company**, **StreetAddress**, **City**, **State**, and **ZipCode**.

■ When finished, complete the command.

▶ *The Save As dialog box appears so you can save the data file.*

■ Type **Customer** in the File Name text box.

■ Specify the drive and directory, if necessary.

■ Complete the command.

▶ *A new document window is opened and a table is inserted, as shown in Figure 3-10.*

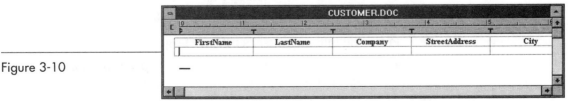

Figure 3-10

Now you need to fill the table and save the file.

■ Type the first field of the first record, **Kay**, and press Tab↹.

■ Type the second field, **Gray**, and press Tab↹.

■ Enter the other five fields. Make sure to press Tab↹ after each.

Buttons & Banners
P.O. Box 2110
Incline Village
NV
89450

▶ *When you press the last Tab↹, a new row for the next record is inserted.*

PRACTICE TIME 3-11

1. Enter the information on four other customers. If a field does not contain information (such as no company name given), just press Tab↹.

George Biehl
Language Technologies
2451 Vegas Valley Drive
Las Vegas NV 89121

Dorothy Durkee
Casino Computers
1255 W. Second Street
Reno NV 89502

Ronald Foss
Heritage Products
P.O. Box 320
Minden NV 89423

Ressa Muller

3000 S. State St.
Ukiah CA 95482

You will notice that a field entry can wrap within a cell.

2. Use the Save command to save the data record using the same filename.

Main Document

You are now ready to create a form letter.

■ From the File menu, select Print Merge.

▶ *The Print Merge Setup dialog box appears.*

■ Click on Edit Main Document.

▶ *The document window for the main document is displayed, as shown in Figure 3-11. It includes buttons you need to merge field codes.*

■ Insert today's date and press ↵Enter three times.

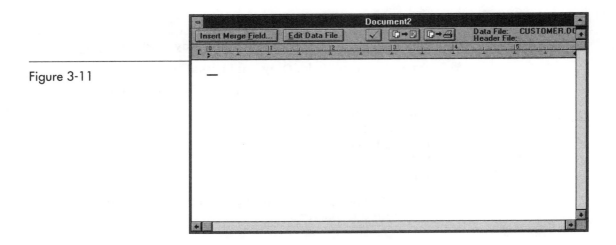

Figure 3-11

The first thing you need to type is the name (first name and last name) of the person you are writing to, followed by the company name one line down, then the street address, and then the city/state/zip on the next line down. This information has to come from the data file.

■ Click on Insert Merge Field.

▶ *The Insert Merge Field dialog box appears, as shown in Figure 3-12, listing all available fields.*

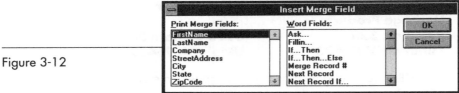

Figure 3-12

■ Select the FirstName field in the Print Merge Fields list box, and then complete the command.

When you enter field codes into a document, these codes are treated as if they are actual words or blocks of text. Any spacing or punctuation you would normally place in the text should be inserted around the code. Here, for example, you want a blank space between the first name and the last name. Hence, you need to place a space between the two codes.

■ Press the (Spacebar).

■ Click on Insert Merge Field.

■ Select LastName and then complete the command.

■ Press (←Enter) to move the insertion point to the next line down.

The second line is to print the company name, which constitutes the third field.

- ■ Click on Insert Merge Field.

- ■ Select Company, and then complete the command.

- ■ Press ⟨←Enter⟩ to go to the next line.

- ■ Similarly, enter StreetAddress on the next line down, and City, State, and ZipCode on the line after. Remember to insert a comma after City.

  ▶ *The screen should read as follows*

  <<FirstName>> <<LastName>>
  <<Company>>
  <<StreetAddress>>
  <<City>>, <<State>> <<ZipCode>>

Next, you need to insert a blank line, and then the salutation should be entered.

- ■ Press ⟨←Enter⟩ twice.

- ■ Type **Dear** and then press ⟨Spacebar⟩, but do not press ⟨←Enter⟩.

To make the letter personal, you will insert the customer's first name here.

- ■ Enter the merge code for FirstName, followed by a colon (:). Press ⟨←Enter⟩.

- ■ Enter the following text. Insert the proper merge code wherever you see <FIRST NAME> or <CITY>.

  If you need $2,000 worth of equipment right away, it's a serious matter. And borrowing money to make the purchase is not always easy. But because you, <FIRST NAME>, have a good credit rating with us, you are now preapproved for a $2,000 credit limit.

  If you are interested, give us a call and one of our sales people will visit you in your fair city of <CITY> right away. Also, if you need more than a $2,000 credit limit, <FIRST NAME>, please let us know. We'll go out of our way to help you any way we can.

  Sincerely,

- ■ Save the file as MAINDOC on the data disk.

You can now begin the merging procedure. This is where the information from the data file is merged into the main document. Microsoft Word will create five letters because there are five records in the data file.

- ■ From the <u>F</u>ile menu, select Print <u>M</u>erge.

■   Click on Merge.

▶   *The Print Merge dialog box is displayed as shown in
Figure 3-13.*

Figure 3-13

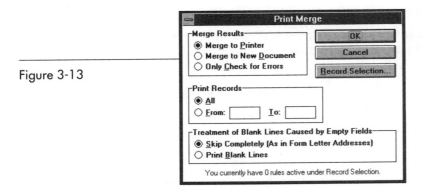

You have three options in merging:

* Merge the main document and data file and print each resulting
merged document.

* Merge the main document and data file and store the resulting
documents in a new file.

* Have Word check the main document and data file and alert you to
errors.

You will do the second option.

■   Click on Merge to New Document.

If you recall, the fifth record, the one for Ressa Muller, did not contain a
company name. To eliminate the blank line caused by an empty field, you
select Skip Completely (As in Form Letter Addresses).

■   Complete the command.

▶   *The form letters appear as a document, as shown in
Figure 3-14.*

Scroll through the form letters. Notice the fifth letter to Ressa Muller. The
blank line (for company name) is eliminated.

You can print these five letters or save the letters as a file. As you can
imagine, the information you can merge in a letter is not just limited to
mailing information. You can include account balance, due date, or any
other information that needs to be personalized. To include any
information, make sure it appears in the data file.

Figure 3-14

ENDING LESSON 3

This is the end of Lesson 3. Exit Microsoft Word and Windows as explained in Lesson 1. There is no need to save changes you made to your files.

S U M M A R Y

In this lesson, many of the terms and concepts that are related to how text appears on the printout are introduced.

☐ **By using the Arrange All command from the Window menu, all document windows are reduced in size and displayed in the window.**

☐ **Copying selected text from one file to another uses the same procedure as copying selected text within a file.**

☐ **Text can be entered flush right, flush left, or decimal-aligned at each tab set.**

☐ **In doing a find or replace, the text can be scanned in either direction starting from the insertion point.**

☐ **Merge requires two files. The first, the main document, contains the form document, along with all codes necessary to tell Microsoft Word what information is to be merged. The second file, a data file, contains records of data that are to be merged into the primary file.**

KEY TERMS

active window   header record   record
data file   left-aligned   replace
field   main document   right-aligned
find   merge   template

COMMAND SUMMARY

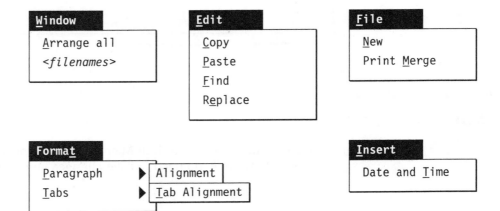

| **Window** |
| Arrange all |
| *<filenames>* |

| **Edit** |
| Copy |
| Paste |
| Find |
| Replace |

| **File** |
| New |
| Print Merge |

Format	
Paragraph ▶	Alignment
Tabs ▶	Tab Alignment

| **Insert** |
| Date and Time |

REVIEW QUESTIONS

1. What is the purpose of arranging windows?

2. What is the difference between the Cut and Copy commands?

3. What does right alignment mean? How do you enter text flush right?

4. What does decimal alignment mean? How do you enter numbers with decimal alignment?

5. What happens if you enter an "up" search with the insertion point at the end of the text?

6. How do you enter the current date in the document?

7. In a find or replace, what is the difference between entering the search text in lowercase and entering it in uppercase?

8. In a find or replace, what happens if you select Match Whole Word Only?

9. In a merge, how do you automatically eliminate blank lines for a field that is empty?

10. What are the two files needed in a merge? Explain the purpose of each file.

EXERCISES

1. Enter the following memo. This exercise also requires you to copy information from the file WD2EX2.

   MEMORANDUM

   DATE: \<current date\>

   TO: **All Employees**

   FROM: **Barbara Pettway**

   SUBJECT: Recipe Contest Winner

   Jackie Copeland, of the Finance Office, was selected the winner of the food contest held at our annual Fall Picnic. The following spaghetti recipe won first prize of $25.

   a. Copy the recipe from file WD2EX2 here. Retrieve WD2EX2 as document 2, and then copy just the recipe. Make sure to include the codes for tab settings.

   b. Add to ingredients at an appropriate location:

      **1/2 cup diced celery
      Parmesan cheese**

   c. Check the spelling.
   d. Save the file on the disk as file WD3EX1.
   e. Print the letter.

2. Enter the following memo. This exercise also requires you to copy information from the file WD1EX3 to paste into this document.

> **MEMORANDUM**
>
> **DATE:**   <current date>
>
> **TO:**   **Market Analysis Department**
>
> **FROM:**   **Charles Jackson, President**
>
> **SUBJECT:** **Water Saddle**
>
> **Al Jenkins of Research has come up with a water saddle that shows some promise.**

a. Copy a block of text from WD1EX3, beginning with "Recently, our department..." and ending with "...which causes chafing." Then type the following paragraph:

> **Please look into the dude ranch market and provide an estimate for product orders over each of the next five years.**

b. Indent both paragraphs 0.5".
c. Check the spelling.
d. Save the file on the disk as WD3EX2.
e. Print the memo.

3. Create the following report.
a. Check the spelling.
b. Save as WD3EX3.
c. Print the report.

CHILD-WATCH SERVICES COMPANY
TRIAL BALANCE
<current date>

Cash (111)	**$1,780.00**	
Accounts Receivable (112)	**1,600.00**	
Equipment (141)	**990.00**	
Buses (143)	**7,400.00**	
Notes Payable (211)		**$7,000.00**
Accounts Payable (212)		**1,470.00**
Janet Escamilla, Capital (311)		**3,300.00**
	$11,770.00	**$11,770.00**

LESSON 4 — Graphics and Columns

OBJECTIVES

Upon completing the material presented in this lesson, you should understand the following aspects of Microsoft Word:

- ☐ **Changing the character size from the Format menu**
- ☐ **Inserting a horizontal line**
- ☐ **Creating newspaper-style columns**
- ☐ **Inserting graphics**

STARTING OFF

Turn on your computer, start Windows, and then launch the Microsoft Word program as you did in previous lessons. Insert your data disk in a disk drive. If necessary, maximize the Word application window.

You will learn to use columns and graphics by creating a newspaper-style document. ***Newspaper-style documents*** have multiple columns on a single page, and text flows from column to column. As you enter text, it fills the first column and then the next column on the same page. When the last column on the page is full, text starts to fill the first column on the next page. When you add or delete text in any of the columns, the remaining text adjusts to keep the columns full. In addition, a newspaper-style document usually has a heading at the top of the first page and some graphics included in the story.

You will create a newsletter, shown in Figure 4-1, for the Sierra Loma Homeowners Association.

Figure 4-1

SIERRA LOMA LOG

Newsletter for Sierra Loma Homeowners Association

October 1993

HOSE BIBS
Many residents have not disconnected their hoses from the outside hose bib because we have had such warm weather. The hose will act as a vacuum and trap the water inside the faucet extension behind the wall. When the water freezes and expands, the pipe may crack under the pressure of the ice. Then when the hose is used, the water runs under your house or into the wall, causing substantial damage. Please disconnect your hoses. Should you have a problem, the Association will not be responsible for either the repair to the hose bib or the resulting damage to your home.

HEAT IN UNOCCUPIED UNITS
 If your unit is left vacant, it is important to leave enough heat so as to prevent your water pipes from freezing. Any subsequent damage resulting from frozen pipes will be the homeowner's responsibility and is not subject to insurance claims.

WINDOW WASHING
The Association has had several inquiries from homeowners wanting their windows washed. The Association does not provide this service. If you check the Yellow Pages, there are several licensed and insured companies available.

MAINTENANCE AND LANDSCAPE
There will be a "skeleton" maintenance crew from November 1, 1993, through March 1994. If we have snow, they will be shoveling it from the walks. For your safety, please do not use salt of any kind on the sidewalks. The snow melts when the salt is applied and refreezes to a slick, icy, and dangerous condition. If you have an area needing "special attention," contact Fred Leisler, maintenance supervisor, at 747-7600.

ASSOCIATION DUES
The monthly homeowner's dues per unit will be raised to $88.00, effective January 1, 1994, to keep up with escalating insurance, utility fees, and maintenance costs.

Remember, the dues must be paid on or before the 1st of each month. There is a $10.00 late fee after the 20th. If you have questions regarding your account or your payment history, feel free to call Barbara Young, bookkeeper for Sierra Loma Homeowners Association.

BOARD MEETING DATES
The Board of Directors meets the third Wednesday of each month at the Clubhouse, starting at 7:00 p.m. All owners are welcome to attend.

There are three basic steps to creating this document.

1. Create the heading (or title).

2. Enter text.

3. Specify the column format.

Any graphics can be inserted either as you enter text or after all text has been entered. You will be saving your document using different filenames at various stages of creation. This way, should you make a mess of the document, you can start from the previous step.

Depending on the font and character size you use, your document may not look the same as shown in this manual. The example in this manual uses various sizes of Times New Roman.

CREATING THE HEADING (TITLE)

You will first insert the text for the title. As you noticed, the title for the newsletter is in characters larger than normal. The character size can be changed by using different sizes as discussed in Lesson 2. You will use 24-point characters.

■ Click on the down arrow next to the size indicator on the ribbon or press Ctrl+P.

■ Select the point size 24.

■ Type **SIERRA LOMA LOG** centered on the line.

P R A C T I C E   T I M E   4 - 1

1. Enter the second line of the title, **Newsletter for Sierra Loma Homeowners Association**. The text is to be centered and entered using 12-point size.

2. Insert three blank lines (press ←Enter four times).

3. Enter the date, **October 1993**, right-justified in 10-point size.

4. Press ←Enter.

5. Make the entire heading bold.

6. Your screen should look similar to Figure 4-2. Save the document as WD4A on your data disk.

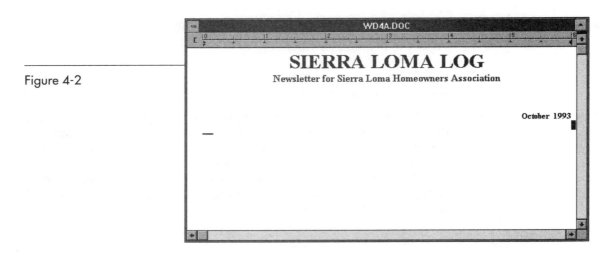

Figure 4-2

INSERTING A HORIZONTAL LINE

You will use the Border command in the Format menu to insert the line.

- Select the entire text.

- From the Forma<u>t</u> menu, select <u>B</u>order.

  ▶ *The Border Paragraphs dialog box, as shown in Figure 4-3, is displayed.*

Click here to draw
lines between the
selected paragraphs

Click here to draw a line above the paragraph

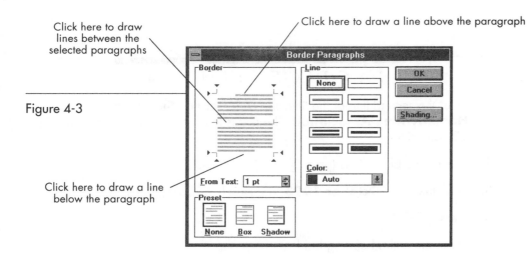

Figure 4-3

Click here to draw a line
below the paragraph

In discussing border options in this lesson, only those options pertinent to the topic being discussed are explained. You may want to explore the rest on your own.

Lines inserted using the Border command are paragraph-oriented. This means these lines are linked, or associated, with the paragraph that was selected (or the one that contains the insertion point) when you entered the Border command. You specify the position of the line by selecting the appropriate portion of the diagram in the Border box, as indicated in Figure 4-3.

■ Specify drawing a line at the bottom of the selected text. To do this, click just below the last line of text in the diagram.

Now, you need to specify the line style in the Line box.

■ Select the second option down on the right-hand column.

■ Complete the command.

■ Position the insertion point below the line and press ⌐←Enter⌐ to insert a blank line.

■ Save the document as WD4B on your data disk.

You will now insert the text for the newsletter. The text will be long enough to cover two columns.

■ Enter the following text in 12-point size.

HOSE BIBS
Many residents have not disconnected their hoses from the outside hose bib because we have had such warm weather. The hose will act as a vacuum and trap the water inside the faucet extension behind the wall. When the water freezes and expands, the pipe may crack under the pressure of the ice. Then when the hose is used, the water runs under your house or into the wall, causing substantial damage. Please disconnect your hoses. Should you have a problem, the <u>Association will not be responsible</u> for either the repair to the hose bib or the resulting damage to your home.

HEAT IN UNOCCUPIED UNITS
If your unit is left vacant, it is important to leave enough heat so as to prevent your water pipes from freezing. Any subsequent damage resulting from frozen pipes will be the homeowner's responsibility and is not subject to insurance claims.

WINDOW WASHING
The Association has had several inquiries from homeowners wanting their windows washed. The Association does not provide this service. If you check the Yellow Pages, there are several licensed and insured companies available.

MAINTENANCE AND LANDSCAPE
There will be a "skeleton" maintenance crew from November 1, 1993, through March 1994. If we have snow, they will be shoveling it from the walks. For your safety, please do not use salt of any kind on the sidewalks. The snow melts when the salt

is applied and refreezes to a slick, icy, and dangerous condition. If you have an area needing "special attention," contact Fred Leisler, maintenance supervisor, at 747-7600.

ASSOCIATION DUES
The monthly homeowner's dues per unit will be raised to $88.00, effective January 1, 1994, to keep up with escalating insurance, utility fees, and maintenance costs.

Remember, the dues must be paid on or before the 1st of each month. There is a $10.00 late fee after the 20th. If you have questions regarding your account or your payment history, feel free to call Barbara Young, bookkeeper for Sierra Loma Homeowners Association.

BOARD MEETING DATES
The Board of Directors meets the third Wednesday of each month at the Clubhouse, starting at 7:00 p.m. All owners are welcome to attend.

■   Save as file WD4C.

CREATING NEWSPAPER-TYPE COLUMNS

Now you are ready to define the columns, but first let's change the view so the true layout of the document is displayed on the screen.

■   From the View menu, select Page Layout.

▶   *The display shows the true layout of the document.*

■   Place the insertion point before the word "Hose" on the first line of text.

■   Click on the column tool button (▦) on the tool bar. You will see a small diagram that represents four columns, as shown in Figure 4-4.

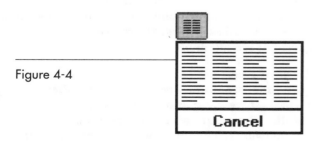

Figure 4-4

■ Click on the second column from the left to indicate two columns.

▶ *The entire document appears in two columns, not just the text from the insertion point down. You can see the result on the Print Preview screen, as shown in Figure 4-5.*

Figure 4-5

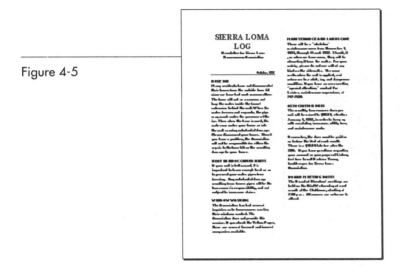

If you want some of the text on a page to be in one-column format and other text in two-column format, the page must be divided into two **sections**—one formatted as one column and the other as two columns. Ordinarily, you would create a section by inserting a section break at the appropriate location and defining the display format for each section. However, right now, you will use the Column command to do both.

■ Click on the column tool and select the first column in the diagram to put the entire document back in one column.

■ Make sure the insertion point is located just before the word "Hose" on the first line of text.

■ From the Format menu, select Columns.

▶ *The Columns dialog box is displayed, as shown in Figure 4-6.*

Figure 4-6

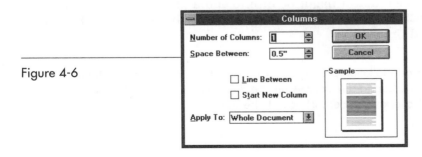

■   Type **2** in the Number of Columns text box.

■   Click on the down arrow beside the Apply To list box.

■   Select This Point Forward and then complete the command.

▶   *The document looks similar to the one shown in Figure 4-7.*

Figure 4-7

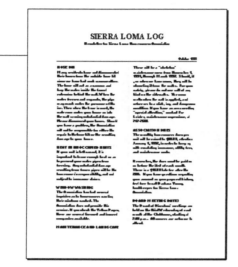

There is one problem with the document as shown in Figure 4-7 (although your document may look a little different). The heading for the article titled "Maintenance and Landscape" appears in one column and the text in the other column. This is not a good format and should be avoided. If your document looks the same as Figure 4-7, place the insertion point at the beginning of this heading and press ⏎Enter as many times as needed to place the heading at the top of the second column.

■   Save the file as WD4D.

ADDING GRAPHICS

You now decide that it might be nice to add a picture. You will insert the picture VICHOUSE.WMF at the beginning of the article titled "Heat in Unoccupied Units."

N O T E :   If the standard installation procedure for Microsoft Word was followed, this picture is available in the Clipart directory within the directory containing Microsoft Word. You may want to check with your instructor to be sure.

■ Place the insertion point at the beginning of the article titled "Heat in Unoccupied Units."

■ From the Insert menu, select Picture.

▶ *The Picture dialog box, as shown in Figure 4-8, is displayed.*

Figure 4-8

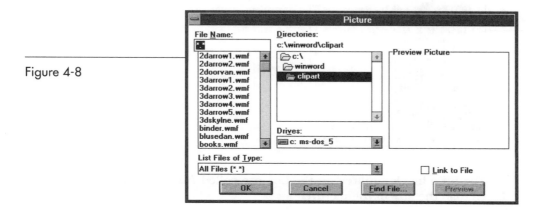

■ Specify the appropriate drive and directory where the Microsoft Word clip art is found.

■ Select the file VICHOUSE.WMF in the File Name list box.

■ Complete the command.

▶ *The picture is inserted at the insertion point position, as shown in Figure 4-9.*

Figure 4-9

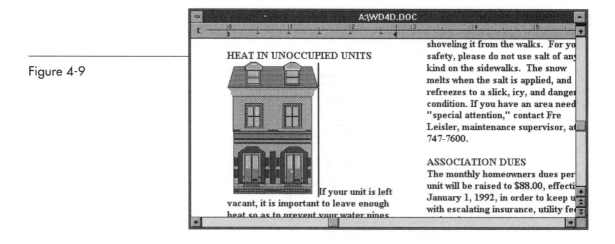

The picture is too big. You can change the size, however.

■ Click on the picture.

▶ *A box appears around the picture, as shown in Figure 4-10.*

Figure 4-10

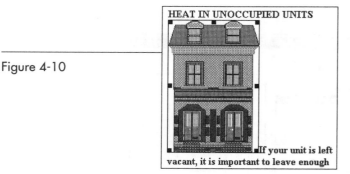

The little black squares on the box are called **handles**. These are used to change the size of the picture.

■ Position the mouse on the lower right handle and drag the handle slightly up and to the left until the picture is about half the original size.

You might notice that the area to the right of the picture is left blank because text is not "wrapping around" the picture. You can change this, too.

■ Make sure the picture is still selected.

■ From the Insert menu, select Frame.

▶ *The text now wraps around the picture, as shown in Figure 4-11.*

Figure 4-11

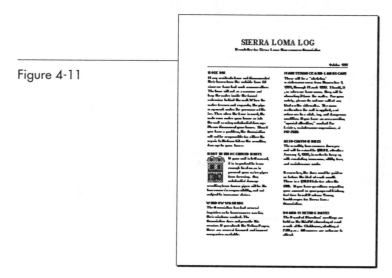

NOTE: If you pressed ⌐←Enter⌐ a couple of times earlier to position the "Maintenance and Landscape" heading in the second column, you may have to delete lines now to adjust.

■   Save your file as WD4E.

■   Print the document.

ENDING LESSON 4

There are many more features to Microsoft Word, such as tables and macros to name two. These should be explored on your own. Remember, the only way to learn to use a word processor is by working on the computer.

Exit Microsoft Word and Windows as explained in Lesson 1. There is no need to save changes you made to your file.

SUMMARY

In this lesson, the terms and concepts related to creating a newspaper-type document are introduced.

☐   **Three basic steps in creating newspaper-type documents are:**
   • **Create the title.**
   • **Enter text.**
   • **Define the format.**

☐   **A line can be inserted in a document using the Border command in the Format menu.**

☐   **A graphic can be inserted in a document as text is being entered or after all text has been entered.**

☐   **A graphic can be sized using the lower right handle.**

KEY TERMS

handles
newspaper-style document
section

COMMAND SUMMARY

Format
Border
Columns

Insert
Picture
Frame

View
Page layout

REVIEW QUESTIONS

1. What is a newspaper-style column?

2. How can you change the size of characters?

3. Explain the steps involved in inserting a horizontal line using the Border command.

4. What does it mean to say that the lines inserted using the Border command are paragraph-oriented?

5. When using the column tool button to specify the number of columns, how do you indicate two columns?

6. How do you include both one-column and two-column text within a page?

7. When you insert a graphic, where is it inserted within a document?

8. How do you change the size of a graphic?

9. What is meant by "wrap text around picture"?

10. What command do you give to make text wrap around a graphic?

EXERCISES

1. Create the document shown in Figure 4-12. Save the document as WD4EX1.

Figure 4-12

Association for Computer Professionals
Tonopah chapter

OCTOBER MEETING

October 24, 1993
Cactus Tavern
178 Main Street
Tonopah, NV
374-9786

Cocktails 6 p.m.

Dinner 7 p.m. - Lasagna

Meeting 8 p.m.

Cost $15.00 per person

****

President
 David Allen

Vice President
 Susan Moore

Secretary
 Michael Stoker

Treasurer
 Chris Boyle

Program Chair
 Ellen Wells

Membership Chair
 Gary Johnson

TOPIC FOR OCTOBER MEETING

"The Emerging Role for Expert Systems"

The development of expert system technologies is probably the most practical and profitable area of development coming out of studies in artificial intelligence. The book The Rise of the Expert Company gives new impetus to the search for areas in which expert systems can be applied to important business and organizational problems. Expert system shells are computer programs that facilitate the development of expert systems. The discussion will focus on typical applications of expert systems, their value, the characteristics of problems that are effectively dealt with by such systems, and the types of shells that can be acquired commercially.

CHAPTER GOSSIP COLUMN
Gary Courtney and his wife, Susan, are expecting a baby. Give some advice to the nervous father-to-be.

Alex Breuder and Barbara Jones got married last month.

Stu Coles is back full-time at his consulting business. You can reach him at 374-3442.

CALENDAR OF EVENTS
November 8 - Board meeting
November 28 - General meeting
December 15 - Christmas Party

2. Create the document shown in Figure 4-13. The graphic is DISK35.WMF in the Clipart directory of the MS Word directory. Save the document as WD4EX2.

Figure 4-13

Care and Handling of Floppy Disks

 You must use proper care in handling floppy disks. They are very fragile. Here are some suggestions for their care and handling:

-   Insert the disk in the disk drive access window (for 5-1/4") or disk drive metal (for 3-1/2") end first, label side up.
-   For 5-1/4" disks, always keep the disk in its envelope when not in use.
-   For 3-1/2" disks, never open the mechanical shutter while a disk is out of the drive. Doing this exposes the surface to dirt, dust, fingerprints, etc.
-   Do not touch the surface of the disk through the access window or wipe the surface with rags or tissue paper.
-   Do not let disks collect dust.
-   Keep disks out of the sun and away from other sources of heat, which can cause them to warp or lose data.
-   Keep disks at least 2 feet away from magnetic fields, such as those generated by electrical motors, radios, televisions, tape recorders, library theft detectors, and other devices. A strong magnetic field will erase information on a disk.
-   When writing on a disk label already attached to the disk, use only a felt-tipped pen. Never use any sort of instrument with a sharp point. Also, never use an eraser. Eraser dust is abrasive and may get on the mylar surface.
-   Keep disks at room temperature before use (a disk just brought in from a cold blizzard has shrunk enough in size that its tracks are not where the system expects to find them).
-   Never open the drive door or remove a disk while the drive is running--that is, while the red in-use light on the front of the disk drive is on. If you do, you can damage the data on your disk.
-   Check to make sure that the gummed tab and external labels are on securely.

3. Create the document shown in Figure 4-14. The graphic is HNDWRTNG.WMF in the Clipart directory of the MS Word directory. Save the document as WD4EX3.

Figure 4-14

CAMPUS COMPUTER CLUB
WEEKLY NEWSLETTER

Volume 5, No. 2   **October 7, 1993**

SEMESTER DUES DUE
Fall semester dues of $5.00, to help cover the cost of computer paper and online file storage, are due by October 10. A fee of $10.00 will be assessed to those who are late with dues.

FALL WORKSHOP SCHEDULE
Due to a mix-up in scheduling with the Computer Science Department's seminars, the Campus Computer Club seminars schedule published last week is void. Please stay tuned for a revised schedule.

IMPORTANT ANNOUNCEMENT
Anyone attempting to infect the campus computer with a worm or virus will be prosecuted. See next item for related info.

SEMINAR SPEAKER
FBI agent Mort Merriweather will speak next Friday at 3 p.m. on computer bugs, worms, and viruses. Mort has been involved in several federal investigations of computer chaos. He says he will give some hints on keeping personal computers "well" and will show us some examples of destructive viruses (including the penalties that their perpetuators incurred).

THIS WEEK'S TIP
Keep your files in order. Use the TIDY_FILE utility written by Kitty Hawkins to delete obsolete versions that clutter disk space. See Chet Williams in the Lab for details.

TWENTY YEARS AGO
Randy Kondo's father has provided us with a newsletter that the computer club published in 1969. An enlarged photocopy is available in our office for those of you interested in stone-age computing. To wit:

The IBM 1620 in use has a memory size of 20,000 characters.

Users can submit one job <u>per day</u> on punched cards.

The new card reader reads 10 cards per second.

The newsletter doesn't say it, but there are no magnetic tape drives, and there is no online storage for student programs or data.

The programming languages most used are FORTRAN IV and Assembler.

The newsletter is typed, get this, using a manual typewriter!

Word for Windows Projects

PROJECT 1

Enter the following text, get a printout, and save the file as WDPROJ1.

MEMORANDUM

DATE: <current date>

TO: **Dallas Irving, President**

FROM: **Keiko Pitter**

SUBJECT: **Water Saddle Market Evaluation**

Our recent survey of market prospects for the water saddle yielded the following conclusions.

1. **The projected sales for five years should be about 1,600 saddles.**

2. **The dude ranch market is but one of three viable markets. Private owners and horseback riding stables are other strong markets.**

3. **It is important to get in first with a quality product. Potential buyers are very conservative. If our initial product has serious flaws, all our subsequent products will not sell.**

4. **Cowpokes, Inc., is currently well positioned to enter this market.**

Some details of our findings include the following items.

Breakdown by Market and Year

YEAR	MARKET			
	Dude Ranches	Privates	Horse Rides	Total
1	50	100	50	200
2	100	100	50	250
3	150	100	50	300
4	200	100	100	400
5	250	100	100	450
Total	750	500	350	1600

Consumer Concerns about a New Product

* Is it produced by a company that can be relied upon?
* Does it represent an improvement, not just a trendy twist?
* Is it reasonably priced?
* Is it durable?

Consumer Suggestions for Product

1. Exhibit at shows. This idea seems so different, people may not realize its value without trying it out.

2. Custom designs. Some interviewees suggested that water saddles might be useful for parades. If they could special order saddles to match their existing tack, this would create another viable market.

PROJECT 2

1. Create the following data file to be used in a merge. Save it as PRJ2DATA. The following fields are needed.

Field 1	Borrower		Field 7	City
Field 2	Lender		Field 8	State
Field 3	Principal		Field 9	Day
Field 4	Payment		Field 10	Month
Field 5	Date		Field 11	Year
Field 6	Rate			

2. Enter the following data in the data file.

Field 1	**Marty Python**	Field 1	**Roni Andrews**
Field 2	**Bank of Arizona**	Field 2	**Bank of Nevada**
Field 3	**$100,000**	Field 3	**$67,000**
Field 4	**$1,300**	Field 4	**$612.88**
Field 5	**December 11, 1993**	Field 5	**October 14, 1993**
Field 6	**10%**	Field 6	**10.5%**
Field 7	**Phoenix**	Field 7	**Reno**
Field 8	**Arizona**	Field 8	**Nevada**
Field 9	**11**	Field 9	**14**
Field 10	**November**	Field 10	**September**
Field 11	**1993**	Field 11	**1993**

3. Create the following main document to be used in a merge. Save the file as PRJ2MAIN. Insert the proper merge codes as indicated.

Promissory Note

The <BORROWER> agrees to pay <LENDER> the principal sum of <PRINCIPAL>. By this note, <BORROWER> agrees to make monthly installments in the sum of <PAYMENT> or more, until said obligation is paid in full. The first payment is due on or before <DATE>, and all successive payments are due on the first day of each succeeding month thereafter until paid in full.

This obligation shall bear interest on the declining principal balance at a rate of <RATE> per annum. In the event the undersigned fails to make a required payment within 30 days when due, then the remaining balance of the obligation shall become due and payable in full. Furthermore, if <BORROWER> is more than 30 days late on a required payment, <LENDER> can elect to recover the collateral securing this obligation, as described below, and dispose of same in any commercially reasonable manner, applying the proceeds of such sale toward the balance remaining hereon.

Additional payments or prepayment in full may be paid by <BORROWER> without penalty.

No delay on the part of <LENDER> in the exercise of any right or remedy shall operate as a waiver thereof, and no

single partial exercise by the same of any right or remedy shall preclude further exercise of any right or remedy.

The obligation evidenced hereby has been made in <CITY>, <STATE>, and shall be governed by the laws of the State of <STATE>.

Dated this <DAY> day of <MONTH>, <YEAR>.

_____

<BORROWER>, borrower

_____

<LENDER>, lender

4. Merge to a new document and get a printout.

Microsoft Word for Windows 2.0 Command Summary

This section is a quick reference for Microsoft Word commands covered in this manual. This is *not* a complete list of all Microsoft Word commands.

Task	Menu Command	Keystroke Shortcut
Alignment	Format, Paragraph	
Centered		Ctrl+E or ▤
Justified		Ctrl+J or ▤
Left-aligned		Ctrl+L or ▤
Right-aligned		Ctrl+R or ▤
Appearance	Format, Character	
Bold		Ctrl+B or 𝐁
Italic		Ctrl+I or 𝐼
Underline		Ctrl+U or 𝐔
Arranging windows	Window, Arrange All	
Column	Format, Columns	▦
Copy text	Edit, Copy	Ctrl+C or ▣
Cut text	Edit, Cut	Ctrl+X or ✂
Date, inserting current	Insert, Date and Time	
Display nonprinting characters	Tools, Options	¶
Display actual layout	View, Page Layout	
Exit Word	File, Exit	Alt+F4
Find text	Edit, Find	
Font	Format, Character	Ctrl+F
Frame, insert	Insert, Frame	
Hanging indent		ruler

Task	Menu Command	Keystroke Shortcut
Help index	Help, Index	`F1`
Insert a horizontal line	Format, Border	
Line indentation	Format, Paragraph	ruler
Line spacing	Format, Paragraph	
Margin settings	Format, Page Setup	ruler
Merge documents	File, Print Merge	
Open existing document	File, Open	`Ctrl`+`F12` or 📂
Open new document	File, New	🗋
Page numbering	Insert, Page Numbers	
Paging	Insert, Break	`Ctrl`+`↵Enter`
Paragraph indentation		ruler
Paste text	Edit, Paste	`Ctrl`+`V` or 📋
Pictures, insert	Insert, Picture	
Preview a file	File, Print Preview	▣
Print a file	File, Print	`Ctrl`+`⇧Shift`+`F12` or 🖨
Replace text	Edit, Replace	
Save file with new name	File, Save As	`F12` or 💾
Save file with same name	File, Save	`⇧Shift`+`F12`
Size of characters	Format, Character	`Ctrl`+`P`
Speller	Tools, Spelling	✔
Tabs	Format, Tabs	ruler
Thesaurus	Tools, Thesaurus	`⇧Shift`+`F7`
Undo typing	Edit, Undo Typing	`Ctrl`+`Z` or ▨
Windows, switching	Window, filename	

Glossary

active window   The window to which the next command will apply. If a window is active, its title bar changes color to differentiate it from other windows.

align   To line up.

application window   A window that contains a running application. The name of the application appears at the top of this window.

border   The outer edge of a window.

byte   A single character.

cascade   A way of arranging open windows on the desktop so that they overlap one another, with the title bar of each window remaining visible.

centered   Text that is centered line by line on the page.

characters per inch (cpi)   The size measurement used for monospaced fonts.

check box   A small square box that appears in a dialog box and that can be selected or cleared. When the check box is selected, an X appears in the window.

click   To press and release a mouse button quickly.

Clipboard   The temporary storage location used to transfer data between documents and between applications.

close   To remove a document window or application window from the desktop.

collapse a directory   To "hide" additional directory levels below a selected directory.

configuration   The arrangement of hardware and software in a computer system.

control-menu box   The icon that opens the control menu for the window. It is always at the left of the title bar.

current directory   The directory that is currently highlighted in the directory tree or whose directory window is the active window.

cursor   A symbol or flashing underscore that shows the position on the screen where an entry will be made.

cut   To remove selected text from a document and place it temporarily on the Clipboard; it can then be pasted to a new location.

data file   In a merge operation, the file that contains the data to be merged into the main document.

default   A value action or setting that is automatically used when no alternative instructions are given. For example, the default drive is where the program looks for data files unless explicitly instructed otherwise.

desktop   The screen background for Windows on which windows, icons, and dialog boxes appear.

dialog box   A rectangular box that either requests or provides information. Many dialog boxes present options to choose among before Windows can carry out a command. Some dialog boxes present warnings or explain why a command can't be completed.

dictionary   A list of correctly spelled words used by Word to check spelling in documents.

directory   A file or a part of a disk that contains the names and locations of other files on the disk.

directory tree   A graphic display in File Manager of the directory structure of a disk.

document window A window within an application window that contains a document you create or modify by using an application. There can be more than one document window in an application window.

double-click To rapidly press and release a mouse button twice without moving the mouse. Double-clicking usually carries out an action, such as opening an icon.

drag To move an item on the screen by holding down the mouse button while moving the mouse.

drop-down list box A single-line dialog box that opens to display a list of choices.

drop-down menu The sub-option menu that appears when an option in the menu bar is highlighted.

endmark An underscore that shows the end of the document.

expand directory To show currently hidden levels in the directory tree.

field A distinct data element used in the merge feature. Each record in a data file is composed of fields.

file A collection of data records with related content; data stored as a named unit on a peripheral storage medium such as a disk.

filename The name assigned a file; it must be no more than eight characters long, and may include an optional extension of a period plus up to three characters.

find A utility that allows you to look for all occurrences of specific words or characters in a document.

first-line indent marker A symbol on the ruler that indicates how far the first line of a paragraph is to be indented.

font The appearance of characters on your screen and printout, which is determined by the typeface, size, and special treatment such as bold, underline, italics, and so on.

format a disk To prepare a blank disk to receive data.

function keys Keys ($\boxed{F1}$ to $\boxed{F10}$ or $\boxed{F12}$) that allow special functions to be entered with a single keystroke.

gray scale The ability to show colors as various shades of gray.

group A collection of programs in Program Manager. Grouping your programs makes them easier to find when you want to start them.

group icon The graphic that represents a Program Manager group that is minimized. Double-clicking the group icon opens the group window.

group window A window that displays the items in a group within Program Manager.

handles Black squares that appear on the box around a graphic that can be used to change the size of the picture.

hanging indent Text layout in which the first line of a paragraph is flush left, while runover lines are indented.

hard page break A page break code that is specially inserted into the text.

header record In a merge, the first row of the data file where field names appear. The header record acts as column headings for the information on the data file.

I-beam The form taken by the mouse pointer when it is in the text area.

icon A graphic representation of various elements in Windows, such as disk drives, files, applications, and documents.

inactive window Any open window that you are not currently working in.

insert mode An editing mode in which the characters you type are inserted at the insertion point, pushing previous characters to the right.

insertion point A blinking vertical bar that indicates where text will be inserted when you next type a character.

justified   Text that is aligned on both the left and right margin.

launching   Starting an application program. This is usually done by double-clicking on the application icon.

left-aligned   Text that is aligned on the left margin.

left indent marker   A symbol on the ruler that shows how far the text is to be indented from the left margin.

list box   Within a dialog box, a box listing available choices—for example, the list of all available files in a directory. If all the choices won't fit, the list box has a vertical scroll bar.

main document   The file containing the document in a merge operation. Using the merge feature, you can print multiple copies, each incorporating data in the data file.

maximize button   The small box containing an up arrow at the right of the title bar. It can be clicked to enlarge a window to its maximum size.

menu   A list of items, most of which are Windows commands. Menu names appear in the menu bar near the top of the window.

menu bar   The horizontal bar containing the menu choices.

merge   A feature that allows you to make personalized documents by inserting the data from a data file into specified positions in the main document.

minimize button   The small box containing a down arrow at the right of the title bar. It can be clicked to shrink a window to an icon.

monospaced characters   Characters in a font in which all letters have the same width.

mouse   A cursor-control device that resembles a small box on wheels. As the box is rolled on a flat surface, the movement of the wheel signals the computer to move the cursor on the display screen in direct proportion to the movement of the mouse.

multitasking   The ability to run more than one application at a time without interrupting the execution of any of the active applications.

newspaper-style document   Text format in which there are multiple columns on a single page. Text flows from column to column.

nonprinting characters   Special characters entered into a document to indicate where certain keys, such as ⏎Enter and Tab↹, were pressed. These characters are not displayed when the document is printed.

open   To display the contents of a file in a window or to enlarge an icon to a window.

paste   To insert text from the Clipboard to a new location in a document. *See* cut.

pathname   The direction to a directory or file within your system. For example, C:\DIR1\FILEA is the pathname for the FILEA file in the DIR1 subdirectory on drive C.

point   To move the pointer on the screen until it rests on the item you want to select.

points   The unit of measure commonly used to indicate font size. A point is 1/72nd of an inch.

pointer   The arrow-shaped cursor on the screen that indicates the position of the mouse.

previewing   The feature that allows you to view the text on the screen as it will be printed.

program group   *See* group.

proportionally spaced characters   Characters in a font that uses varying widths for different letters; for example, an *m* is wider than an *i*, as it is here.

record   A single block of data used in the merge feature. Each block of data fields pertaining to a separate person or item is a record in the data file.

replace   A utility that searches for all occurrences of specific words or characters and replaces them with words or characters you specify.

restore button   The small box at the right of the title bar that contains a down arrow and an up arrow. The restore button appears after you have enlarged a window to its full size. It can be clicked with a mouse to return the window to its previous size.

ribbon A section of the window that contains buttons that let you change the way text looks.

right-aligned Text that is aligned on the right margin.

right indent marker A symbol on the ruler that shows how far the text is to be indented from the right margin.

ruler The bar at the top of the workspace that displays current settings for margins, tabs, justification, and spacing.

scroll To move through a document by moving lines off the top or bottom of the screen. Word does this automatically as you enter text, or you can scroll through a document using the scroll bar.

section A portion of the text. A section can be as short as a single paragraph or as long as an entire document. Each section can be formatted differently.

selection bar An unmarked area along the left side of the text area. It is used to select text with the mouse. When the mouse pointer is in the selection bar, it turns into a right-pointing arrow.

soft font A font that is downloaded to your printer's memory from a disk provided by the font's manufacturer.

soft page break A page break that is inserted automatically by the program, based on specified margin and page depth settings.

soft return A line break that is inserted automatically by the program, based on specified margin settings.

status bar A horizontal bar at the bottom of the document window that displays such information as the font style and type size being used and the insertion point position.

subdirectory A directory contained within another directory. All directories are subdirectories of the root directory.

tabs Settings that determine indents, or the new position of the insertion point each time you press Tab⇆; by default, tabs are set at every half-inch.

task An open application.

template A special document you can use as a pattern to create other documents of the same type.

text area The area below the ruler in which you enter text or graphics.

text box A box within a dialog box where you type information needed to carry out the chosen command.

tile A way of arranging open windows so that windows do not overlap, but all windows are visible. Each window takes up a portion of the screen.

title bar The horizontal bar located at the top of a window and containing the title of the window.

toggle A command that alternately turns a feature on and off.

tool bar A section of the window that contains buttons with icons, called tools, that you can click on to perform certain operations.

typeface The graphic style applied to characters; common typefaces are Courier, Helvetica, and Times Roman. The typeface is often referred to as the font.

typeover mode An editing mode that replaces the character the insertion point is on with the character you type. It is active when the letters "OVR" appear in the status bar.

window A rectangular area on your screen in which you view an application or document.

wordwrap A feature that prevents splitting a word at the end of a line on the screen; instead, the word is placed intact on the next line.

workspace The area of a window between the menu bar and the status bar, which displays the document you are working with or information about the application you are working on.

Index